# Contents

# Introduction

What makes handmade birthstone jewelry so special? Perhaps it's the symbolism. Ancient peoples felt certain stones were more powerful during certain months of the year; the stones later became associated with the people born in those months, creating the birthstone tradition we know and adding a layer of meaning to an already lovely object. Then again, maybe it's the individualized nature of the jewelry that makes it so extraordinary. When you make birthstone jewelry for yourself, you know you have a perfect fit, and made as a gift, it demonstrates a personal touch.

This collection of 38 jewelry projects features beautiful necklaces, bracelets, and earrings from *BeadStyle* magazine, including 13 all-new jewelry sets. Each chapter features three stylish and eye-catching projects, as well as information about the physical traits, history, and lore of the traditional birthstones and popular alternatives for each month. Clear instructions and full-color photos guide you through each step, making it fast and easy to create gorgeous jewelry.

You can substitute different birthstones into most designs in this book – try making Helene Tsigistras's "Rock crystal drops" bracelet (p. 40) with aquamarine or topaz briolettes instead of crystal quartz for a colorful alternative. Or make Brenda Schweder's "Edgy sapphire dangles" (p. 76) in shades of green for a May or August birthday. Plus, the Year-round chapter (p. 106) features two additional projects that can be personalized and adapted easily for a special person or a special event.

Whether you love the authenticity of genuine gemstones or crave the sparkle of cost-effective alternatives, options abound, including faceted glass, crystal, and dyed quartz. Soon you'll be making beautiful, custom jewelry in a wide variety of styles for everyone you know – and yourself, too!

| MONTH | TRADITIONAL BIRTHSTONE | SECONDARY BIRTHSTONE |
|---|---|---|
| January |  garnet |  rose quartz |
| February |  amethyst |  onyx |
| March |  aquamarine |  bloodstone |
| April |  diamond |  crystal quartz/rock crystal |
| May |  emerald |  chrysoprase |
| June |  pearl |  moonstone |
| July |  ruby |  carnelian |
| August |  peridot |  sardonyx |
| September |  sapphire |  lapis lazuli |
| October |  opal |  pink tourmaline |
| November |  topaz |  lemon quartz |
| December |  turquoise |  blue topaz |

# Materials &

bead tips

bead caps

two-strand bead

multistrand spacer bars

jump ring

soldered jump ring

split ring

cone

spacers

assorted clasps

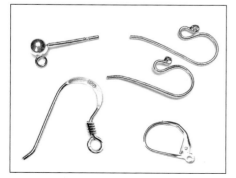

earring findings

crimp beads and crimp covers

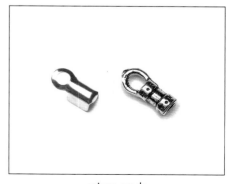

crimp ends

# Tools

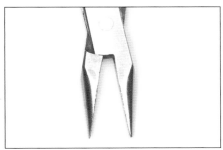
chainnose pliers

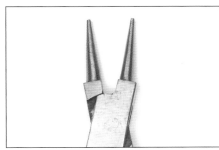
roundnose pliers

crimping pliers

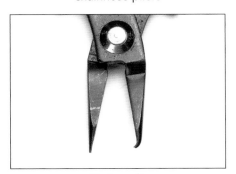
split-ring pliers

wire cutters

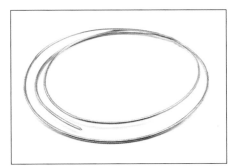
wire

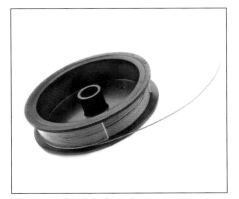
flexible beading wire

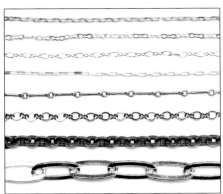
chain

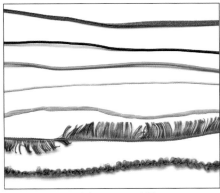
cords, ribbons, and fibers

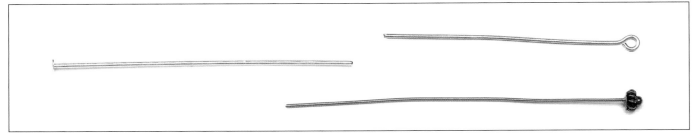
head pin, eye pin, and decorative head pin

# Basics

## LOOPS AND JUMP RINGS

### PLAIN LOOP

**1** Trim the wire or head pin ⅜ in. (1cm) above the top bead. Make a right-angle bend close to the bead.

**2** Grab the wire's tip with roundnose pliers. The tip of the wire should be flush with the pliers. Roll the wire to form a half circle. Release the wire.

**3** Reposition the pliers in the loop and continue rolling.

**4** The finished loop should form a centered circle above the bead.

### WRAPPED LOOP

**1** Make sure you have at least 1¼ in. (3.2cm) of wire above the bead. With the tip of your chainnose pliers, grasp the wire directly above the bead. Bend the wire (above the pliers) into a right angle.

**2** Using roundnose pliers, position the jaws vertically in the bend.

**3** Bring the wire over the top jaw of the roundnose pliers.

**4** Reposition the pliers' lower jaw snugly into the curve. Wrap the wire down and around the bottom of the roundnose pliers. This is the first half of a wrapped loop.

**5** Position the chainnose pliers' jaws across the loop.

**6** Wrap the wire tail around the wire stem, covering the stem between the loop and the top bead. Trim the excess wire and press the cut end close to the wraps with chainnose pliers.

### SET OF WRAPS ABOVE A TOP-DRILLED BEAD

**1** Center a top-drilled bead on a 3-in. (7.6cm) piece of wire. Bend each wire upward to form a squared-off "U" shape.

**2** Cross the wires into an "X" above the bead.

**3** Using chainnose pliers, make a small bend in each wire so the ends form a right angle.

**4** Wrap the horizontal wire around the vertical wire as in a wrapped loop. Trim the excess wrapping wire.

## OPENING AND CLOSING LOOPS OR JUMP RINGS

**1** Hold the loop or jump ring with two pairs of chainnose pliers or chainnose and roundnose pliers, as shown.

**2** To open the loop or jump ring, bring one pair of pliers toward you and push the other pair away. String materials on the open loop or jump ring. Reverse the steps to close the open loop or jump ring.

## OPENING SPLIT RINGS

Slide the hooked tip of a pair of split-ring pliers between the two overlapping wires.

# CRIMPS

## FLATTENED CRIMP

**1** Hold the crimp using the tip of your chainnose pliers. Squeeze the pliers firmly to flatten the crimp.

**2** Tug the wire to make sure the crimp has a solid grip. If the wire slides, repeat the steps with a new crimp.

## FOLDED CRIMP

**1** Position the crimp bead in the notch closest to the crimping pliers' handle.
**2** Separate the wires and firmly squeeze the crimp.

**3** Move the crimp into the notch at the pliers' tip and hold the crimp as shown. Squeeze the crimp bead, folding it in half at the indentation.
**4** Test that the folded crimp is secure.

## FOLDED END CRIMP

**1** Glue one end of the cord and place it in a crimp end. Use chainnose pliers to fold one side of the crimp end over the cord.

**2** Repeat with the second side of the crimp end and squeeze gently.

# KNOTS

## OVERHAND KNOT

Make a loop and pass the working end through it. Pull both ends to tighten the knot.

## SURGEON'S KNOT

Cross the left end over the right end and go through the loop. Go through again. Pull the ends to tighten. Cross the right end over the left end and go through once. Pull the ends to tighten.

# January

## Garnet

**Physical properties**

Garnets are durable gemstones commonly known for their deep, wine-red color. Some unusual varieties of garnets include brown, green, yellow, and orange shades. Found in Africa — particularly Kenya, Namibia, and Madagascar — and in India, Sri Lanka, Thailand, Brazil, Canada, the United States, the Czech Republic, and Spain, garnets are cut into a wide variety of shapes and sizes, including beads and cabochons. The stones are sometimes dyed to intensify their color; dyed stones should be rinsed to remove excess surface dye. It is best to clean them with warm, soapy water and a soft brush.

**History and lore**

Many cultures see garnets as a warrior's stone and set them in shields or buckles — in fact, many Crusaders wore garnets in hopes that the stones would protect them on their way home. According to legend, Noah used a garnet lantern on the ark, and centuries later, Eastern Europeans thought garnets would ward off vampires. The name comes from the Latin word *granatus* (grain- or seed-like), because the rich red color resembles pomegranate seeds. Garnets symbolize fire, faith, fidelity, and constancy and are believed to stimulate blood flow and prevent lethargy.

## Rose Quartz

**Physical properties**

Rose quartz is known for its cloudy translucent pink or peach color. Found in Brazil, Madagascar, the United States, Russia, and Scotland, artists can carve this fairly hard stone into many different shapes.

**History and lore**

In ancient times, Romans gave rose quartz as a gift of love, and one myth says that Aphrodite's blood colored the stone pink. Because of this, rose quartz is associated with love, friendship, healing, beauty, opening the wearers' hearts, and helping them to love themselves and receive love from others.

# Garnets and gold

This gleaming crimson necklace features faceted garnet briolettes and bicone crystals with vermeil accents. Complete the ensemble with a delicate pair of earrings for a look that's timeless and sophisticated.

**by Rupa Balachandar**

**1** **necklace** • Determine the finished length of your necklace. (This necklace is 17 in./ 43cm.) Add 6 in. (15cm) and cut a piece of beading wire to that length.
String briolettes until the strand is half the desired length. Center the briolettes on the wire, and position them in opposite directions, as shown.

## Supply List

**necklace**
- 16-in. (41cm) strand 5 x 8mm or larger garnet briolettes
- **40–50** 4mm bicone crystals
- **4** 4mm flat spacers
- flexible beading wire, .014 or .015
- **2** crimp beads
- box clasp
- chainnose or crimping pliers
- diagonal wire cutters

**earrings**
- **2** 5 x 8mm or larger garnet briolettes
- **6** 4mm bicone crystals
- 6 in. (15cm) 26-gauge half-hard wire
- **4** 1½-in. (3.8cm) head pins
- pair of 3-in. (7.6cm) earring threads with open jump rings
- chainnose pliers
- roundnose pliers
- wire cutters

**2** String a spacer on each end. String bicone crystals on each end until the strand is within 1 in. (2.5cm) of the desired length.

**3** On each end, string a bicone, a spacer, a crimp bead, a bicone, and half of a clasp. Go back through the beads just strung and tighten the wire. Check the fit, and add or remove an equal number of beads from each end if necessary. Crimp the crimp beads (see Basics, p. 8) and trim the excess wire.

**1** **earrings** • To make a briolette dangle, cut a 3-in. (7.6cm) piece of wire. String a briolette and make a set of wraps above the bead (Basics).

**2** String a bicone crystal and make a wrapped loop (Basics) perpendicular to the briolette.

**3** To make a bicone dangle, string a bicone on a head pin. Make a wrapped loop. Repeat to make a second bicone dangle.

**4** Open the loop (Basics) of an earring thread and attach a bicone dangle, the briolette dangle, and a bicone dangle. Close the loop. Make a second earring to match the first.

# Clustered garnet earrings

**by Stacey Yongue**

Tiny garnets dangle from wire-wrapped jump rings in these ingenious earrings. Although the earrings are small, they make a big impact. Experiment with differently shaped garnets and jump rings to find a style that suits you.

**1** On a head pin, string a garnet bead. Make the first half of a wrapped loop (see Basics, p. 8). Make nine garnet units.

**2** On a bench block or anvil, hammer a 9–11mm jump ring. Turn the jump ring over and hammer the other side.

## Supply List

- **18** 3–4mm garnet beads
- **16 in.** (41cm) 26-gauge wire
- **18** 1½-in. (3.8cm) head pins
- **2** 9–11mm soldered jump rings
- **2** 5–6mm jump rings
- **2** 3–4mm soldered jump rings
- pair of earring wires
- chainnose pliers
- roundnose pliers
- wire cutters
- bench block or anvil
- hammer

### EDITOR'S TIP
For an organic look, wrap the wire loosely around the stem when completing the wraps on each garnet unit.

**3** Cut an 8-in. (20cm) piece of 26-gauge wire. Wrap the wire tightly around two-thirds of the jump ring. Trim the excess wire. Use chainnose pliers to tuck the ends in.

**4** Attach a garnet unit to the unwrapped section of the jump ring. Complete the wraps. Repeat with the remaining garnet units.

**5** Open a 5–6mm jump ring (Basics). Attach the wrapped jump ring and a 3–4mm jump ring. Close the jump ring.

**6** Open the loop (Basics) of an earring wire. Attach the dangle and close the loop. Make a second earring to match the first.

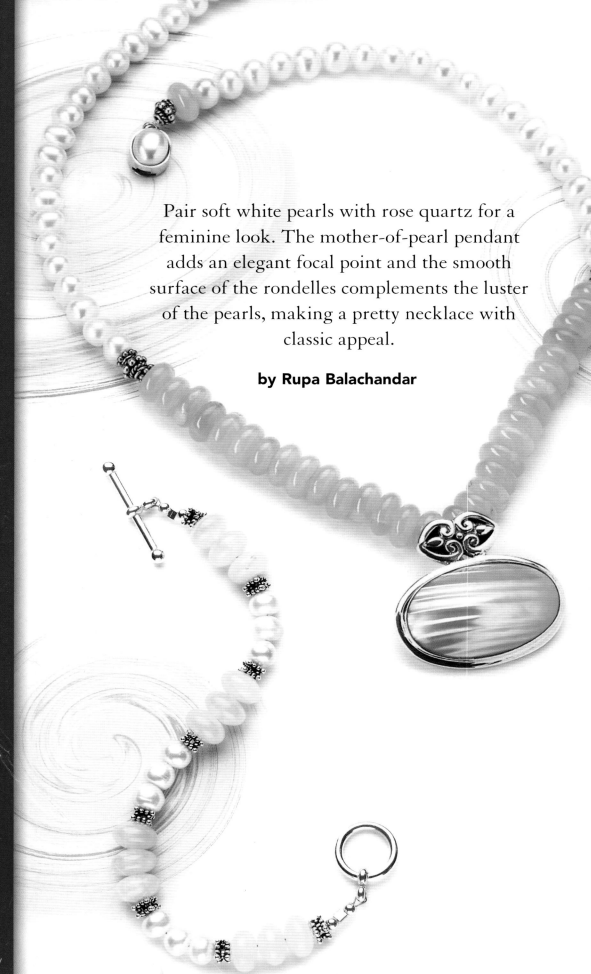

# Romantic rose quartz

Pair soft white pearls with rose quartz for a feminine look. The mother-of-pearl pendant adds an elegant focal point and the smooth surface of the rondelles complements the luster of the pearls, making a pretty necklace with classic appeal.

**by Rupa Balachandar**

**1 necklace •** Determine the finished length of your necklace. (This one is 18 in./46cm.) Add 6 in. (15cm) and cut a piece of beading wire to that length. String a few seed beads onto the wire. Center the pendant on the wire, placing it over the seed beads.

**2** String 15 quartz rondelles on each side of the pendant.

**3** String a flat spacer, a bicone spacer, a flat spacer, and 20 pearls on each end.

**4** On each end, string a rondelle, a bicone, a crimp bead, a 3mm round, and half of a clasp. Go back through the last beads strung and tighten the wire. Check the fit and add or remove an equal number of beads from each end, if necessary. Crimp the crimp beads (see Basics, p. 8) and trim the excess wire.

## Supply List

**necklace**
• mother-of-pearl pendant
• 16-in. (41cm) strand white button pearls, 5-6mm
• 16-in. strand rose quartz rondelles, 10 x 4mm
• **4** 5mm bicone spacers
• **4** 5mm flat spacers
• **4-6** size 11º seed beads
• flexible beading wire, .014 or .015
• **2** crimp beads
• **2** 3mm round beads
• clasp
• chainnose or crimping pliers
• diagonal wire cutters

**earrings**
• **2** pearls left over from necklace
• **2** rondelles left over from necklace
• **2** 5mm flat spacers
• **2** 2-in. (5cm) head pins
• pair of earring wires
• chainnose pliers
• roundnose pliers
• diagonal wire cutters

**bracelet**
• **9** pearls left over from necklace
• **12** rondelles left over from necklace
• **8** flat spacers, 5 x 5 x 3mm square
• flexible beading wire, .014 or .015
• **2** crimp beads
• **4** 3mm round spacers
• clasp
• chainnose or crimping pliers
• wire cutters

**1 earrings •** String a pearl, a flat spacer, and a rondelle on a head pin. Make a wrapped loop (Basics) above the top bead.

**2** Open an earring wire, attach the unit, and close the wire. Make a second earring to match the first.

**1 bracelet •** Determine the finished length of your bracelet, add 5 in. (13cm), and cut a piece of beading wire to that length. String a spacer, three rondelles, a spacer, and three pearls. Repeat this pattern until the bracelet is the desired length, ending with a spacer.

**2** On each end, string a 3mm round, a crimp bead, a round, and half a clasp. Go back through the last beads strung. Check the fit and add or remove an equal number of beads, if necessary. Crimp the crimp beads and trim the excess wire.

# February

## Amethyst

### Physical properties

Amethyst's hues range from pale lavender to deep purple, and from opaque to transparent. Russian amethyst, one of the more expensive varieties, is dark and clear, but some opaque amethysts feature stripes and swirls. Heat lightens the color of amethyst, and can even turn it into citrine (a yellow stone). Since heat and light affect the color of the stone, it should be stored in a dark place, but otherwise amethyst is a fairly hard gemstone and easy to care for. It can be found in many locations in South America, Africa, and Russia, and because this gemstone is so widely available, it's very affordable.

### History and lore

Many cultures have long prized the rich purple pigment of amethyst, often considered to be the color of royalty. According to Greek mythology, the stone was created when a maiden named Amethyst or Amethystos fled the god Dionysus, and begged Artemis for assistance. Artemis granted her wish by turning her to stone, and Dionysus poured wine over her as a tribute, dyeing the stone purple. Because of this myth, it is believed that amethyst protects its wearer from intoxication. Amethyst is also believed to evoke calmness, and so is a symbol of peace and serenity.

## Onyx

### Physical properties

Mysterious black onyx is a wonderful stone. Found all over the world, it is inexpensive, and, because it also is a fairly hard stone, it is easy to care for. Onyx is easy to cut and carve, so it is available in all kinds of interesting shapes and sizes, from large cabochons to tiny faceted beads. The term "onyx" usually refers to the solid black color of this quartz gemstone, but other varieties may be gray, reddish, or banded, and often are known by other names, such as gray chalcedony or sardonyx.

### History and lore

The Greeks and Romans valued banded onyx, with its layers of black and white, because it was perfect for carving cameos and intaglios. The Romans thought the stone enhanced courage, and Middle Easterners and Europeans used it to guard against sorcery during the Middle Ages. In modern times, the stone is thought to encourage new beginnings, allowing the wearer to change bad habits, and release old relationships or bad feelings.

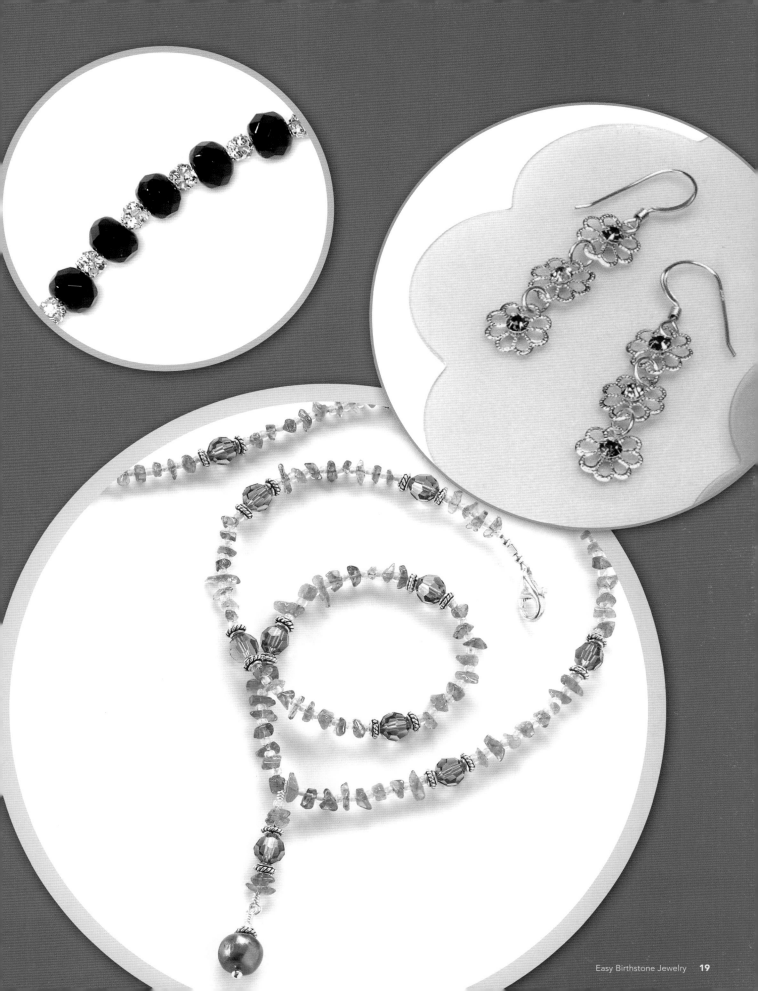

# Amethyst chips & crystals

A liberal dose of amethyst chips gives lighthearted appeal to a graceful necklace. The gemstone chips are easy to match with seed beads, crystals, and pearls to produce a mellow, monochromatic palette. The necklace pattern translates easily to matching earrings or a quick bracelet.

**by Maria Camera**

**1** necklace • To make the dangle's bottom unit, string a focal bead, a flat spacer, and a seed bead on a head pin. Make the first half of a wrapped loop (see Basics, p. 8) above the top bead.

To make the dangle's top unit, cut a 3½-in. (9cm) piece of 22-gauge wire. Make a wrapped loop at one end. String two gemstone chips, a spacer, a crystal, a spacer, two chips, and a seed bead. Make a wrapped loop perpendicular to the bottom loop.

**2** Attach the dangle's bottom unit to the bottom loop of the dangle's top unit. Complete the wraps.

**3** Determine the finished length of your necklace. (This one is 17 in./43cm.) Add 6 in. (15cm) and cut a piece of beading wire to that length. Center the dangle on the wire.

On each side of the dangle, string an alternating pattern of eight chips and eight seed beads, a spacer, a crystal, and a spacer. Repeat on each end until the necklace is within 1 in. (2.5cm) of the desired length.

**4** On one end of the strand, string a 2mm round, a crimp bead, a round, and a soldered jump ring. Go back through the last beads strung. Repeat on the other end, substituting a lobster claw clasp for the soldered jump ring. Tighten the wires, check the fit, and add or remove an equal number of beads from each end, if necessary. Crimp the crimp beads (Basics) and trim the excess wire.

bracelet • Determine the finished length of your bracelet, add 5 in. (13cm), and cut a piece of beading wire to that length. Repeat the pattern in step 3 of the necklace until the bracelet is within 1 in. (2.5cm) of the desired length. Follow step 4 to finish the bracelet.

**1** earrings • Make a dangle following steps 1 and 2 of the necklace.

**2** Open the loop (Basics) of an earring wire and attach the dangle. Close the loop. Make a second earring to match the first.

## SupplyList

**necklace**
- 8-12mm focal bead
- 16-in. (41cm) strand 3-5mm amethyst chips
- **9-13** 6mm round crystals
- 1g size 11º seed beads
- **4** 2mm round spacers
- **19-27** 4mm flat spacers
- 3½ in. (9cm) 22-gauge half-hard wire
- 2-in. (5cm) 22-gauge decorative head pin
- flexible beading wire, .014 or .015
- **2** crimp beads
- lobster claw clasp and soldered jump ring
- chainnose pliers
- roundnose pliers
- diagonal wire cutters
- crimping pliers (optional)

**bracelet**
- 3-5mm amethyst chips
- size 11º seed beads
- **3-5** 6mm round crystals
- **4** 2mm round spacers
- **6-10** 4mm flat spacers
- flexible beading wire, .014 or .015
- **2** crimp beads
- lobster claw clasp and soldered jump ring
- chainnose or crimping pliers
- diagonal wire cutters

**earrings**
- **2** 8-12mm focal beads
- **8** 3-5mm amethyst chips
- **2** 6mm round crystals
- **4** size 11º seed beads
- 7 in. (18cm) 22-gauge half-hard wire
- **2** 2-in. 22-gauge decorative head pins
- **6** 4mm flat spacers
- pair of earring wires
- chainnose pliers
- roundnose pliers
- wire cutters

Rather than using expensive clear amethyst, try a lovely crystal flower alternative. These charms highlight the look of amethyst at its purple pinnacle. For a two-tone look, alternate light and dark amethyst. To get into the mixed-metal trend, assemble a pattern of crystals set in both gold and silver charms.

**by Tyrenia Pyskacek**

**1** **bracelet** • Open a 4mm jump ring (see Basics, p. 8) and attach: an amethyst flower charm, and a light amethyst flower charm. Close the jump ring.

**2** Alternating colors, continue to link charms with jump rings until the bracelet is within ½ in. (1.3cm) of the desired length. Attach a lobster claw clasp to one end with a jump ring. Attach a 5mm jump ring to the other end.

# SupplyList

**bracelet**
- **12–16** 9mm crystal flower charms: **6–8** amethyst, **6–8** light amethyst (Rings & Things, rings-things.com)
- **13–17** 4mm oval jump rings
- lobster claw clasp and 5mm oval jump ring
- **2** pairs of chainnose pliers

**earrings**
- **6** 9mm crystal flower charms: **4** amethyst, **2** light amethyst
- **4** 4mm oval jump rings
- pair of earring wires
- chainnose pliers
- roundnose pliers

## CUFF-STYLE BRACELET

To make a 7-in. (18cm) cuff, you will need 56 crystal flower charms, 106 oval jump rings, and a four-strand slide clasp.

**1.** Make 14 columns of four crystal charms each by linking charms and jump rings.

**2.** Connect the charms in one column to the respective charms in the next column until all columns are connected.

**3.** On each end, use one jump ring each to attach each of the two middle flowers to their respective loops on a slide clasp. Attach two jump rings together to attach the outer flowers to the outer loops of the slide clasp.

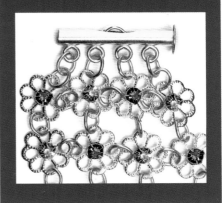

**1** **earrings** • Open two jump rings, and attach an amethyst flower charm to each side of the light amethyst flower charm. Close the jump rings.

**2** Open the loop (Basics) of an earring wire and attach the dangle. Close the loop. Make a second earring to match the first.

# Striking onyx collection

This monochromatic set is easy to string but still provides maximum style. Sleek crescent-shaped and faceted onyx beads are highlighted by sparkling bicones and rhinestone balls in an eye-catching display.

**by Helene Tsigistras**

**1 necklace •** Determine the finished length of your necklace. (This one is 19 in./48cm.) Add 6 in. (15cm), and cut a strand of flexible beading wire to that length. String a crimp bead and half of a clasp, and go back through the crimp bead. Crimp the crimp bead (see Basics, p. 8), and trim the excess wire.

**2** String a rhinestone ball and the first hole of an onyx crescent bead.

**3** String: bicone crystal, onyx rondelle, bicone, and the second hole of the crescent bead.

**4** Repeat steps 2 and 3 until the necklace is within 1½ in. (3.8cm) of the desired length, ending with a rhinestone ball.

String a crimp bead and the other half of the clasp, go back through the crimp bead, and tighten the wire. Check the fit, add or remove beads if necessary, and crimp the crimp bead. Trim the excess wire.

**1 bracelet •** Determine the finished length of your bracelet, add 6 in. (15cm), and cut the strand of flexible beading wire to that length. String a crimp bead and half of a clasp. Go back through the crimp bead and crimp the crimp bead.

**2** Starting with a rhinestone ball, string an alternating pattern of rhinestone balls and onyx rondelles until the bracelet is within 1 in. (2.5cm) of your desired length, ending with a rhinestone ball.

String a crimp bead and the other half of the clasp and go back through the crimp bead. Crimp the crimp bead and trim the excess wire.

**1 earrings •** Cut a 5 in. (13cm) piece of silver flexible beading wire. Center a rondelle, two bicones, and a crescent bead on the wire.

**2** String a crimp bead over both ends of the wire, and take both ends back through the crimp bead, forming a loop. Use roundnose pliers to hold the loop in place and tighten the wire. Crimp the crimp bead and trim the tails.

**3** Gently open a rhinestone ball and cup it around the crimp bead. Use your fingers or chainnose pliers to close the ball around the crimp bead. Open the loop (Basics) of an earring finding and attach the earring. Make a second earring to match the first.

## Supply List

**necklace**
• 16-in. (41cm) strand 20 x 15mm crescent-shaped onyx beads
• 16-in. (41cm) strand 10mm onyx faceted rondelles
• **20 or more** 5mm rhinestone balls
• **38 or more** 4mm bicone crystals
• flexible beading wire, .012–.015
• clasp
• **2** crimp beads
• crimping pliers
• wire cutters

**bracelet**
• **18** 10mm onyx faceted rondelles
• **19** 5mm rhinestone balls
• flexible beading wire, .012–.015
• clasp
• **2** crimp beads
• crimping pliers
• wire cutters

**earrings**
• **2** 20 x 15mm crescent-shaped onyx beads
• **2** 10mm onyx faceted rondelles
• **2** 5mm rhinestone balls
• **4** 4mm bicone crystals
• silver beading wire, .012–.015
• pair of decorative earring findings
• roundnose pliers
• chainnose pliers (optional)
• crimping pliers
• wire cutters

# March

## Aquamarine

### Physical properties

Aquamarine ranges in color from pale blue to deep blue green, and from clear to semi-opaque. Heat treatments bring out the blue color, and the color and clarity of the stone determines its value. Like other heat-treated stones, aquamarine can lose its color if exposed to light, so store your jewelry in a dark place and clean the stones with a soft brush and warm, soapy water. Brazil is a primary source for aquamarine, but it is also found in Australia, Madagascar, Russia, Mozambique, India, Afghanistan, and Pakistan. Because aquamarine is one of the more expensive semi-precious stones, faceted glass functions as an economical alternative.

### History and lore

Said to be a gift from mermaids in part because of its lovely sea-blue color, aquamarine is associated with sea travel and considered a lucky stone for sailors. The word *aquamarine* literally means "sea water," and legends about Atlantis mention the stone. Perhaps the prevalent water theme in aquamarine lore tied the stone to the Fountain of Youth – it is also believed to bring eternal youth and good luck to its wearer. Some say aquamarine encourages happiness, frees the wearer from laziness, and provides assorted health benefits.

## Bloodstone

### Physical properties

Bloodstone is a deep opaque green with red or brown inclusions or spots. Common and very inexpensive, this gemstone is found throughout the world, including India, Australia, and the United States. The stone is available in many different bead and cabochon forms, and its polished surface should be protected from scratches.

### History and lore

Many different stories suggest how bloodstone may have been named. Some say the name arose from a belief that the stone strengthens the bloodstream and heart. Other sources report that early Christians associated the red inclusions with the blood from Christ's wounds – it was also known as the martyr's stone in medieval times. Bloodstone is thought to be a healing stone, associated with courage and charity, and believed to attract good fortune and wealth into the wearer's life.

# Aquamarine twist

**by Lea Nowicki**

Two tricks make for a graceful, tapered twist in this dazzling rope necklace made from individual strands of pearls and faceted aquamarine beads. First, select similarly sized pearls and beads to ensure both have equal prominence in the finished piece. Second, align the strands so one extends farther than the other on each end. Save two top-drilled beads for earrings and add a cluster of accent beads to complete this polished jewelry set.

**1** necklace • Determine the finished length of your necklace. (This one is 16 in./41cm.) Add 8 in. (20cm) and cut two pieces of beading wire to that length. On one wire, string 13½ in. (34.3cm) of briolettes or round beads. (For a shorter necklace, string 11 in./28cm of beads.) Make sure each bead faces the opposite direction of the preceding bead.

On the second wire, string pearls to the same length as the previous strand.

**2** On one end of each wire, string 2½ in. (6.4cm) of accent beads. On the other end of each wire, string 1½ in. (3.8cm) of accent beads. (For a shorter necklace, string 2¼ and 1¼ in./5.7 and 3.2cm, respectively.) Reverse one of the strands to stagger the center beads. Tape each end.

**3** Cut a 3½-in. (8.9cm) piece of 22-gauge wire. Make a wrapped loop (see Basics, p. 8) at one end. Repeat. Twist the strands together and check the fit, allowing 1½ in. (3.8cm) for finishing. Remove the tape, and add or remove beads from each end if necessary.

On one end of each strand, string a crimp bead, a round spacer, and the wrapped loop. Go back through the beads just strung plus a few more. Tighten the wires, crimp the crimp beads (Basics), and trim the excess beading wire. Repeat on the other end.

**4** String a cone and a 5mm bead on the wire on one end. Make the first half of a wrapped loop above the bead. Repeat on the other end.

**5** Attach each loop to half of a clasp and complete the wraps.

**1** earrings • String an accent bead on a head pin. Make a plain loop (Basics) above the bead. Repeat to make a total of five dangles.

**2** Cut a 3-in. (7.6cm) piece of wire. String a top-drilled bead and make a set of wrap above it (Basics). String the dangles on the wire.

**3** Make a wrapped loop above the dangles. Open the loop (Basics) of an earring wire and attach the dangle. Make a second earring to match the first.

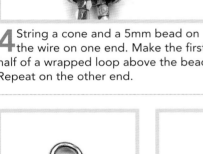

# SupplyList

**necklace**
- 16-in. (41cm) strand top-drilled aquamarine briolettes or round beads, approx. 6 x 11mm
- 16-in. strand top-drilled pearls, approx. 6 x 9mm
- 16-in. strand 3-4mm silver accent beads
- **2** 5mm round beads
- **2** silver cones, approx. 11 x 13mm
- **4** 2-3mm round spacers
- 7 in. (18cm) 22-gauge half-hard wire
- flexible beading wire, .014 or .015
- **4** crimp beads
- toggle clasp
- chainnose pliers
- roundnose pliers
- wire cutters

**earrings**
- **2** top-drilled aquamarine beads, left over from necklace
- **10** silver accent beads, left over from necklace
- **10** 1-in. (2.5cm) head pins
- 6 in. (15cm) 26-gauge half-hard wire
- pair of earring wires
- chainnose pliers
- roundnose pliers
- wire cutters

# Cascading aquamarine

The faceted gemstones and crystals of this tiered necklace capture the light like waves of the sea. The light colors and silver rings give this sparkling necklace an airy feel.

**by Helene Tsigistras**

**1** On a 4-in. (5cm) piece of wire, make the first half of a wrapped loop (see Basics, p. 8), attach a soldered jump ring, and complete the wraps.

**2** String a disk bead above the wraps and begin a wrapped loop. Attach a 15mm ring, and complete the wraps.

# Supply**List**

- 16-in. strand 12mm faceted aquamarine disk beads
- **52** 6mm aquamarine bicone crystals
- **6** 15mm rings
- **4** 12mm rings
- 4 ft. (1.2m) 22-gauge wire
- **4** soldered jump rings
- flexible beading wire, .012–.015
- **2** crimp beads
- toggle clasp
- chainnose pliers
- roundnose pliers
- crimping pliers (optional)
- wire cutters

**3** On a new 4 in. piece of wire, start a wrapped loop and attach the other side of the ring. Finish the wrapped loop. String a disk bead.

**4** Make the first half of a wrapped loop, attach 15mm ring, and complete the wraps.

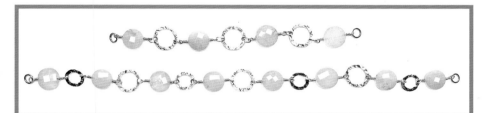

**5** Repeat steps 3 and 4 to add another disk bead and ring. Repeat a second time, but substitute a soldered jump ring for the 15mm ring.
Make a second chain as you did the first, but alternate 12mm and 15mm rings until your chain is eight disk beads long. End with a soldered jump ring on each end.

**6** Determine the finished length of your necklace. (This one is 21 in./53cm.) Add 6 in. (15cm) and cut a piece of flexible beading wire to that length.
Center an alternating pattern of six bicones and five disk beads on the wire. String a bicone and one jump ring from the short chain on each side.

**7** On each end, string two bicones, a disk bead, two bicones, and the jump ring from each end of the long chain.

**8** On each end, string two bicones and a disk bead. String a pattern of four bicones and a disk on each end until the necklace is within 1 in. (2.5cm) of the desired length. End with bicones.

**9** String a crimp bead, a clasp half, and a crimp bead on each end. Go back through the crimp beads, and check the fit. Add or remove an equal number of crystals from each side if necessary. Crimp the crimp beads (Basics) and trim the excess wire.

# Basic bloodstone set

Join earth-tone rounds and nuggets in an easy necklace with casual appeal. The autumn-hued bloodstone beads are almost universally flattering — a perfect fit for every wardrobe.

**by Helene Tsigistras**

**1** necklace • String an 8mm round bead and a spacer on a head pin and make a wrapped loop (see Basics, p. 8) above the beads.

**2** Cut a 4-in. (10cm) piece of wire and make the first half of a wrapped loop at one end. Attach the bead unit and finish the wraps.

**3** String a spacer, nugget, and a spacer. Make a wrapped loop above the beads.

## Supply List

MAR

**necklace**
- **3** 20mm bloodstone nuggets
- 16 in. (41cm) strand 8mm round bloodstone beads
- **15** 4mm spacers
- 2-in. (5cm) 22-gauge head pin
- 4 in. (10cm) 22-gauge half-hard wire
- flexible beading wire, .012–.015
- **2** crimp beads
- toggle clasp
- chainnose pliers
- roundnose pliers
- crimping pliers (optional)
- wire cutters

**bracelet**
- 16 in. (41cm) strand 20mm bloodstone nuggets
- flexible beading wire, .012–.015
- **2** crimp beads
- toggle clasp
- crimping pliers
- wire cutters

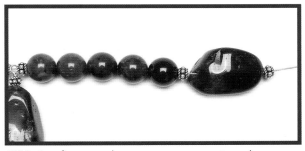

**4** Determine the finished length of your necklace. (This one is 18 in./46cm.) Add 6 in. (15cm), and cut a strand of flexible beading wire to that length. Center the pendant and two spacers on the wire.

**5** String five rounds, a spacer, a nugget, and a spacer on each end.

**6** On each end of the necklace, string an alternating pattern of five rounds and one spacer until the necklace is within 1½ in. (3.8cm) of the desired length. End with a spacer.

**7** On each end, string a crimp bead, a spacer, and half a clasp. Go back through a few beads and check the fit, adding or removing beads from both ends, if necessary. Tighten the wire and crimp the crimp beads (Basics). Trim the excess wire.

**1** bracelet • Determine the finished length of your bracelet, add 6 in. (15cm), and cut a strand of flexible beading wire to that length. String a crimp bead and half of a clasp. Go back through the crimp bead and crimp the crimp bead.

**2** String nuggets until your bracelet is within 1 in. (2.5cm) of the desired finished length.
String a crimp bead and the other half of the clasp. Go back through the crimp bead, and check the fit. Add or remove beads, if necessary. Crimp the crimp bead, and trim the excess wire.

**EDITOR'S TIP**
Curve the bracelet into a circle before crimping so there is enough room for the beads to sit gracefully. If the beads are too tight, the bracelet will be stiff.

# April

## Diamond

### Physical properties

Famed as the hardest stone in the world, diamonds are made of pure carbon, and should be stored and cleaned separately, since they can scratch other jewelry – and each other. The highest quality diamonds are perfectly clear and colorless, but there are variations in a range of colors (the colors come from impurities in the stone). Because they are so precious, you won't find natural jewelry-grade diamonds as beads (why would you want to drill out the center to make a hole?), but many substitutes exist, including cubic zirconium, rhinestones, and clear or "white" crystals.

### History and lore

These days, most people associate diamonds with love — they are the most popular stones for engagement rings. The name comes from the Greek word for invincible, and diamonds were once believed to protect the wearer from injury or poison and assist with honesty and clarity. They also are associated with brain health and memory.

## Crystal Quartz

### Physical properties

This member of the quartz family is ideally clear and colorless, though some specimens have milky white inclusions. Because quartz is a hard stone, jewelers, manufacturers, and artists cut it in a variety of shapes, including both round and faceted beads. Crystal quartz is widely available, but the price varies, depending on the quality of the stones.

### History and lore

Also called rock crystal, crystal quartz is associated with water and with mental clarity — think of the expression "crystal clear." In fact, the name "crystal" comes from the Greek word *krystallos*, meaning ice. Some believe the stone enhances the purity and calmness of the wearer and helps him or her focus.

# Diamond collar

Diamonds may be a girl's best friend, but rhinestones can be a low-maintenance gal pal. Easy on your wallet and even easier to slide on a pretty ribbon, fun and sparkly rhinestone letters spell out initials, names, or messages. So add a little bling to your look with this personalized necklace and bracelet.

**by Naomi Fujimoto**

**1** necklace • Apply nail polish or Fray Check to one end of the ribbon and let it dry. String the ribbon through each rhinestone letter in the desired order.

Center the middle letter (or letters) on the ribbon, leaving about ⅛ in. (3mm) between each letter.

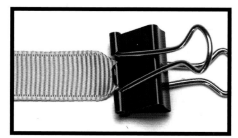

**2** Check the fit by wrapping the ribbon snugly around your neck. Cut the ribbon ½ in. (1.3cm) shorter on each end than the desired length (this necklace is 13 in./33cm plus the extender).

Apply glue to one end and fold each corner under slightly, forming a V at the end. Clamp with a clothespin or clip and let it dry. Repeat on the other end.

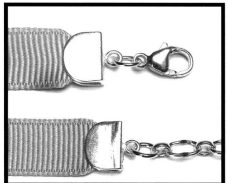

**3** Remove the clips. Insert each ribbon end into a pinch end. Close each pinch end with chainnose pliers. (To avoid marring, put a cloth between your pliers and the pinch end.)

**4** Open a jump ring (see Basics, p. 8) and go through a pinch end loop and the end link of a 3-in. (7.6cm) chain. Close the jump ring.

Use a jump ring to attach a lobster claw clasp to the remaining pinch end loop.

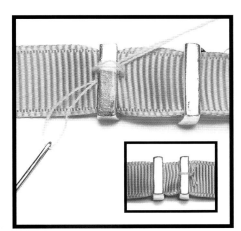

**5** Thread a needle and knot the ends together, leaving a 2-in. (51mm) tail. To tack down each letter, pass the needle through the ribbon and around the bar on the back of a letter twice. Make sure the stitches are not visible on the front of the ribbon. Tie a surgeon's knot (Basics) and trim the ends to ⅛ in. (3mm).

**bracelet** • Follow the instructions for the necklace, determining the finished length (step 2) by wrapping the ribbon around your wrist. Omit the chain in step 4 and finish that end with a jump ring.

# Supply**List**

**necklace**
- 14mm rhinestone slide letter(s)
- 1½ ft. (46cm) or more ½-in. (1.3cm) grosgrain or other sturdy ribbon
- 3 in. (7.6cm) chain for extender
- **2** 10 x 11mm pinch ends
- lobster claw clasp
- **2** jump rings
- clothespins or binder clips
- sewing needle
- thread to match ribbon color
- **2** pairs chainnose pliers or chainnose and roundnose pliers
- scissors
- diagonal wire cutters
- clear nail polish or Dritz Fray Check
- E6000 glue

**bracelet**
- 14mm rhinestone slide letter(s)
- 6 in. (15cm) or more ½-in. grosgrain or other sturdy ribbon
- **2** 10 x 11mm pinch ends
- lobster claw clasp
- **2** jump rings
- clothespins or binder clips
- sewing needle
- thread to match ribbon color
- **2** pairs chainnose pliers or chainnose and roundnose pliers
- scissors
- wire cutters
- clear nail polish or Dritz Fray Check
- E6000 adhesive

# Glittering briolette necklace

Achieve the elegant look of diamonds without the expense. Beautiful crystal-clear briolettes and bicones add sparkle and drama to a necklace fit for a walk down the red carpet, or perhaps just a night on the town.

**by Helene Tsigistras**

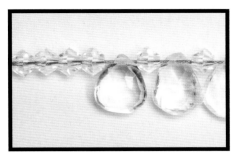

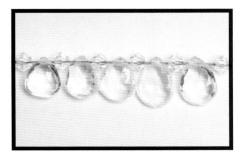

**1** **necklace** • Determine the finished length of the shortest strand of your necklace. (This one is 20 in./51cm.) Add 6 in. (15cm), and cut a strand of flexible beading wire to that length. Add 8 in. (20cm) and cut a second piece of flexible beading wire to that length. On the short wire, string five 3mm crystal bicones, an alternating pattern of crystal drops and 3mm bicones for 6 in., and five more 3mms.

**2** Center the beads on the strand. Center 9 in. (23cm) of the alternating crystals and 3mms on the second strand.

## SupplyList

**APR**

**necklace**
- 16-in. strand 6mm faceted crystal briolettes, clear
- **2** 6mm bicone crystals, clear
- **80** 4mm bicone crystals, clear
- **75** 3mm bicone crystals, clear
- 6–8 5mm silver spacer beads
- flexible beading wire, .012–.015
- **2** crimp beads
- toggle clasp
- crimping pliers
- wire cutters

**earrings**
- **6** 6mm crystal briolettes, clear
- **6** 4mm bicone crystals, clear
- 6 in. (13cm) 3mm cable chain
- **2** 5mm oval jump rings
- **6** 1½ in. (3.8cm) 24-gauge head pins
- 18 in. (46cm) 24-gauge half-hard wire
- pair of earring wires
- chainnose pliers
- roundnose pliers

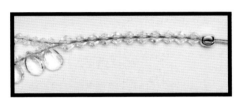

**3** String a 6mm bicone, 10 4mm bicones and a silver bead over both wires on each end.

String an alternating pattern of 10 4mms and a silver bead on each end until you are within 1 in. (2.5cm) of the desired length, ending with bicones.

**4** String a crimp bead and half of a clasp on each end of the necklace. Go back through the crimp beads, tighten the wires, and check the fit. Remove an equal number of bicones from each side, if necessary. Crimp the crimp beads (see Basics, p. 8), and trim the excess wire.

**1** **earrings** • Cut three lengths of chain: ¾ in. (1.9cm), 1 in. (2.5cm), and 1⅛ in. (2.9cm). Open a jump ring (Basics), and attach the three chains to an earring finding in the order desired. Close the jump ring.

**2** String a 4mm bicone crystal on a head pin and make the first half of a wrapped loop (Basics). Make a total of three bicone units.

**3** String a briolette on a 3 in. (5cm) piece of wire and make a set of wraps (Basics) above it. Make the first half wrap of a wrapped loop above the wraps. Make three briolette units.

**4** Attach each of the briolette units to the bottoms of a chain, and complete the wraps.

**5** Count up six links from the bottom of a chain and attach a bicone unit. Complete the wraps. Repeat with the other two bicone units. Make a second earring to match the first.

# Rock crystal drops

These luscious teardrops allow light to dance off every little facet. The beads nestle together for an interesting strand, but the design is easy. When you have beads like these, you can simply string them, and the effect will be breathtaking.

**by Helene Tsigistras**

**1** bracelet • Determine the finished length of your bracelet. Add 5 in. (13cm), and cut a strand of flexible beading wire to that length. String a spacer, a crimp bead, and half of a clasp. Go back through the crimp bead and spacer, and crimp the crimp bead (see Basics, p. 8).

**2** String briolettes until the bracelet is within 1 in. (2.5cm) of the desired length. Make sure the briolettes are nestled together. String a spacer, a crimp bead, and the other half of the clasp. Go back through the crimp bead and spacer, check the fit, and crimp the crimp bead. Trim the excess wire.

**EDITOR'S TIP**
To ensure that the bracelet hangs gracefully, instead of sitting stiffly on the wrist, curve the bracelet into a circle before crimping the last crimp bead. The beads should be able to move a little on the wire.

## SupplyList

**bracelet**
- 12-in. (30cm) strand 10mm faceted teardrop crystal quartz briolettes
- **2** 4mm spacer beads
- flexible beading wire, .012–.015
- **2** crimp beads
- toggle clasp
- crimping pliers
- wire cutters

**earrings**
- **8** 10mm faceted teardrop crystal quartz briolettes
- silver-plated flexible beading wire, .012–.015
- **2** crimp beads
- pair of earring wires
- crimping pliers
- roundnose pliers (optional)
- wire cutters

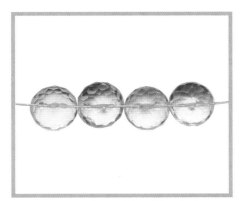

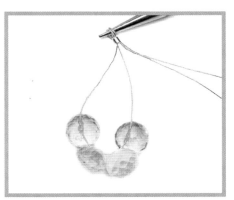

**1** earrings • Cut a 6-in. (15cm) piece of silver-plated flexible beading wire, and center four briolettes on the strand.

**2** String a crimp bead over both wire ends. Go back through the crimp bead, leaving a loop, and tighten the wire around the tip of your roundnose pliers. Crimp the crimp bead. Trim the excess wire. Open an earring wire and attach the loop. Close the earring wire. Make a second earring to match the first.

# May

## Emerald

### Physical properties

Highest-quality emeralds are transparent grass green. The rareness of transparent stones makes them valuable, but opaque inclusions can be useful as an indication of an authentic emerald. Beads and cabochons tend to be more opaque, and therefore more affordable. Because emeralds are so costly, crystals often are used as substitutes. True emeralds are most commonly found in Brazil, Colombia, India, Zambia, and Zimbabwe, and should be handled with care; polish jewelry with a soft cloth and avoid water and extreme temperatures, since emeralds are commonly treated with oils or resins.

### History and lore

Many ancient cultures, including Indians, Incas, Aztecs, and Egyptians, prized emeralds. They are believed to ward off evil and enemies, strengthen the wearer's memory and intelligence, and improve health and well-being and promote emotional balance.

## Chrysoprase

### Physical properties

This opaque stone is a fairly rare member of the chalcedony family, and ranges in color from apple to olive green. Chrysoprase is primarily found in Australia and the United States and is easy to find as reasonably priced beads.

### History and lore

Chrysoprase is believed to repel negativity, releasing physical and emotional stress from the body and acting as a shield against it. Because of its color, it is associated with money and success. During medieval times, it was used to decorate cathedrals and chapels.

# Elegant emerald bracelet

While you can make this multistrand bracelet with any focal bead, an 8mm crystal in a birthstone color provides perfect balance, because the crystal and the spacers above and below are equal in length. Though the cube adds contrast, a bicone or round crystal would be equally appealing. To save on cost, use silver-plated beads.

**by Kathie Scrimgeour**

**1** Determine the finished length of your bracelet, add 5 in. (13cm), and cut three pieces of beading wire to that length.

String two 4mm rounds on the top and bottom wires. String an 8mm crystal on the middle wire. Center the beads on each wire.

**2** On each side of the center beads or crystal on each strand, string three 6mm rounds and a 5mm round. String capsule beads on each end of each wire until each strand is 1 in. (2.5cm) from the desired length.

## SupplyList

- 8mm crystal, emerald
- **10** 4mm round spacers
- **6** 5mm round spacers
- **18** 6mm round spacers
- **36-48** 10 x 3mm silver-plated capsules (Fire Mountain Gems, 800-355-2137, firemountaingems.com)
- flexible beading wire, .014 or .015
- **6** crimp beads
- three-strand clasp
- chainnose or crimping pliers
- wire cutters

**3** On each end of each strand, string a crimp bead, a 4mm round, and the corresponding loop on a clasp half, making sure that the clasp is oriented correctly. Check the fit, and add or remove an equal number of beads from each end of each strand if necessary. Crimp the crimp beads (see Basics, p. 8) and trim the excess wire.

### EDITOR'S TIPS
- Need just a little more length to make it fit? Rather than adding a capsule bead to each end of each strand (20mm total, more than ¾ in.), string a 4mm bead or two (8-16mm total, ⅜-⅝ in.) between the last capsule and the crimp.
- Avoid making a stiff bracelet that is difficult to fasten – curve the bracelet on your work surface and fasten the clasp before you crimp the ends. A little space between beads when the bracelet is laying flat will allow the strands to curve gracefully around your wrist.

# Emerald tiers

Genuine emeralds can be pricey, but emerald-green crystals are a great alternative. The rich green hues of long malachite ovals and sparkly cylinder beads make for a colorful, sculptural jewelry set.

**by Helene Tsigistras**

**1** Determine the finished length of your necklace. (This one is 19.5 in./49.5cm.) Add 15 in. (38cm), and cut a piece of flexible beading wire to that length. Center a cylinder bead on the wire and string a crystal over both ends.

**2** String ten cylinder beads on each end of the wire.

**3** String each end of the wire through one end of a malachite bead, crossing the wires inside the bead.

**4** String ten cylinder beads on each end, and string a crystal over both ends.

**5** Repeat steps 2–4, then repeat steps 2 and 3 again.

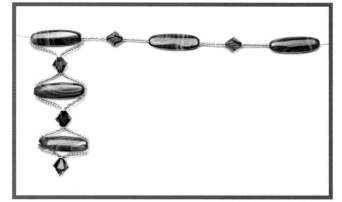

**6** One each end, string 10 cylinder beads and a crystal, then 10 cylinder beads and a malachite bead. Repeat the pattern on both ends until the necklace is within 1 in. (2.5cm) of the desired length, ending with cylinder beads.

**EDITOR'S TIP**
If you can't find 25mm malachite ovals, try a smaller size, such as an 18mm oval, paired with a 6mm bicone crystal. You'll need to add a pattern repetition to each end of the necklace to get the same length, but the results are equally stunning.

## Supply List

- **11** 8mm bicone crystals
- 16-in. (41cm) strand 25mm malachite oval beads
- 4g 11º Japanese cylinder beads, gray luster
- flexible beading wire, .012–.015
- **2** crimp beads
- clasp
- crimping pliers
- wire cutters

**7** On each end, string a crimp bead and half of a clasp. Go back through the crimp bead and tighten the wire. Check the fit, and add or remove and equal amount of beads from each end, if necessary. Crimp the crimp beads (see Basics, p. 8) and trim the excess wire.

The green of chrysoprase can range from bright apple to darker olive, but the natural brown tones of wood beads are always the perfect complement. This necklace and the matching pair of earrings can be assembled in an afternoon.

**by Helene Tsigistras**

**1** **necklace •** Determine the finished length of the shorter strand of your necklace. (The shorter strand of this necklace is 18½ in./47cm.) Add 6 in. (15cm), and cut a strand of flexible beading wire to this length. Cut a second strand of beading wire 10 in. (25cm) longer. Hold the wires together and string a crimp bead and half of a clasp over the ends. Take both ends back through the crimp bead, and crimp the crimp bead (see Basics, p. 8).

**2** String three wood beads and a chrysoprase drop over both wires. Repeat five times.

**3** Separate the strands. On the longer wire, string three wood beads and one drop. Repeat eleven times. String three more wood beads.

**4** On the shorter wire, string about 8 in. (20cm) of wood beads. String a drop bead over both wires. The wood bead strand should sit inside the drop strand. String the pattern of three wood beads and one drop five times. String three wood beads. (The two sides of the necklace should match). String a crimp bead and the second half of the clasp. Go back through the crimp bead, tighten the wire, and crimp the crimp bead. Trim the excess wire.

**1** **earrings •** Cut a 4-in. (10cm) piece of 22-gauge wire. String a chrysoprase drop 1 in. (2.5cm) from one end, and make a set of wraps (Basics) above it with the short wire.

**2** String two wood beads above the wraps, and make a wrapped loop (Basics) above the beads. Open the loop (Basics) of an earring finding and attach the bead unit. Close the loop. Make a second earring to match the first.

## SupplyList

**necklace**
- 16-in. (41cm) strand 10mm chrysoprase drop beads
- **2** 16-in. strands 6mm wood beads
- flexible beading wire, .012–.015
- **2** crimp beads
- hook-and-eye clasp
- crimping pliers
- wire cutters

**earrings**
- **2** 10mm chrysoprase drop beads
- **4** 6mm wood beads
- 8 in. (20cm) 22-gauge half-hard wire
- pair of earring wires
- chainnose pliers
- roundnose pliers
- wire cutters

# June

## Pearl

### Physical properties

Pearls are unique among birthstones because they are created by living creatures. Natural pearls form when an irritant (a grain of sand, for example) finds its way into the shell of a mollusk, such as an oyster. The mollusk secretes nacre, more commonly known as mother-of-pearl, to cover the irritant, and a pearl forms. To create cultured pearls, irritants are purposefully placed in the mollusk and the coating process is monitored. While China and Japan produce the most cultured pearls, Tahiti and Australia produce cultured pearls that are larger in size. Pearls can be dyed or color treated. Finding pearls that match in color, shape, luster, and size is difficult, so enhanced cultured pearls or faux pearls are frequently used as alternatives, especially by those on a tight budget. Treat pearls with care so they don't become scratched or scuffed.

### History and lore

Pearls always have been a popular adornment. They're mentioned in many ancient texts, including *The Odyssey*. Believed to promote purity and good health, pearls are often associated with balancing the body and harmonizing the wearer with the natural world.

## Moonstone

### Physical properties

Moonstone has a unique shimmering glow, reminiscent of moonlight, caused by layers of feldspar growth. When the stone is turned from side to side, the beautiful pearly glow, known as adularescence, seems to roll across the surface; adularescence appears in all varieties of the stone. Moonstone ranges in color from white to gray to peach, while rainbow moonstone reveals many different colors in its glow. Commonly found in India, Australia, the United States, and several other places worldwide, moonstone is a popular material for making beads, cabochons, and bezeled pendants.

### History and lore

Moonstone was once an imperial gemstone of India and is still very popular in many cultures. It is believed to be a calming, stress-reducing stone that opens the mind to new possibilities and increases the wearer's sense of safety and security, providing confidence. The stone is especially connected with women, and is believed to protect women and babies.

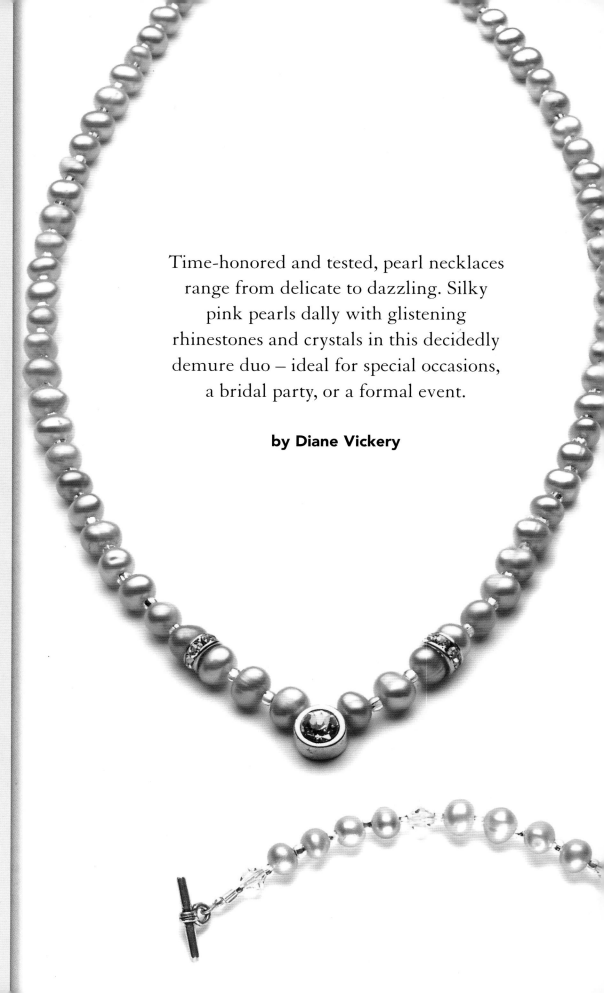

# Demure pearls

Time-honored and tested, pearl necklaces range from delicate to dazzling. Silky pink pearls dally with glistening rhinestones and crystals in this decidedly demure duo – ideal for special occasions, a bridal party, or a formal event.

**by Diane Vickery**

**1** **necklace** • Determine the desired length of your necklace. (This one is 18 in./46cm.) Add 6 in. (15cm), and cut a piece of beading wire to that length.

Center the bezel-set cubic zirconium on the wire. On each end, string three pearls alternating with two seed beads, then a rondelle.

**2** On each end, alternate pearls and seed beads until the necklace is 1 in. (25mm) shorter than the desired length.

**3** String a seed bead, a crimp bead, a seed bead, and one of a clasp's jump rings. Go back through the last beads strung. Repeat on the other end, going through the remaining jump ring. Tighten the wire. Check the fit and add or remove beads as needed. Crimp the crimp beads (see Basics, p. 8) and trim the excess wire.

# Supply List

**necklace**
- bezel-set 5mm cubic zirconium
- **2** 6mm rhinestone rondelles, crystal
- 16-in. (.41m) strand 5mm potato-shaped freshwater pearls
- 2g size 11º seed beads, silver-lined clear
- **2** crimp beads
- hook-and-eye clasp with attached jump rings
- flexible beading wire, .014 or .015
- chainnose or crimping pliers
- wire cutters

**bracelet**
- 16-in. strand 4mm potato-shaped freshwater pearls
- 1g size 11º seed beads, silver-lined clear
- **6** 3mm bicones, crystal
- **2** 6mm rhinestone rondelles, crystal
- 6mm bicone, crystal
- toggle clasp
- **2** crimp beads
- flexible beading wire, .014 or .015
- chainnose or crimping pliers
- wire cutters

**1** **bracelet** • Determine the desired length of your bracelet, add 5 in. (13cm), and cut a piece of beading wire to that length.

Stringing a seed bead before every bead, string a 3mm crystal, a pearl, a rondelle, a pearl, a 6mm crystal, a pearl, a rondelle, a pearl, and a 3mm crystal. String a seed bead at the end. Center these beads on the wire.

**2** On one end, beginning with a pearl, alternate four pearls and four seed beads. String a 3mm crystal and seed bead. Repeat this pattern once more on this end. String the pattern twice on the other end of the wire.

**3** Finish the bracelet as in step 3 of the necklace, using a toggle clasp in place of the hook-and-eye clasp.

# Metallic pearl cascade

Combine different strands of pearls for a striking necklace that highlights the incredible hues of lustrous colored pearls. Whether you choose consistent shapes or opt for more organic-looking pearls, you'll achieve the most dramatic necklace by selecting three contrasting sizes.

**by Teri Bienvenue**

**1** necklace • For the three large-pearl strands: Cut a piece of beading wire (see Basics, p. 8) for the shortest strand of your necklace. (The shortest strand of this necklace is 15½ in./39.4cm.) Cut two more pieces, each 4 in. (10cm) longer than the previous piece. On each wire, string large pearls until the strand is within 4 in. (10cm) of the desired length.

**2** For the three small-pearl strands: Cut a piece of beading wire 2 in. (5cm) longer than the shortest wire in step 1. Cut two more pieces, each 1 in. (2.5cm) longer than the previous piece. On each wire, string small pearls until the strand is within 4 in. (10cm) of the desired length.

**3** For the three medium-pearl strands: Cut a piece of beading wire 4 in. (10cm) longer than the shortest wire in step 1. Cut two more pieces, each 2 in. (5cm) longer than the previous piece. On each wire, string medium pearls until the strand is within 4 in. (10cm) of the desired length.

**4** Cut a 4-in. (10cm) piece of 20-gauge wire. Make a wrapped loop (Basics) on one end. Repeat.

**5** On one end of each strand, string five or six 11º seed beads, a crimp bead, an 11º, and a wrapped loop. Go back through the last few beads strung and tighten the wire. Repeat on the other side. Check the fit, and add or remove beads if necessary, allowing approximately 2 in. (5cm) for finishing. Crimp the crimp beads (Basics) and trim the excess wire.

**6** On each end, string a cone, a bead cap, an accent bead, and a bead cap. Make the first half of a wrapped loop. Attach half of a clasp and complete the wraps.

**EDITOR'S TIP**
When selecting cones for the necklace, note the size of the bottom opening: it must accommodate nine strands of pearls.

# Supply List

**necklace**
- **4** 16-in. (41cm) strands 8–10mm pearls
- **4** 16-in. (41cm) strands 5–6mm pearls
- **4** 16-in. (41cm) strands 2–4mm pearls
- **2** 6–10mm accent beads
- **1g** 11º seed beads
- **4** bead caps
- flexible beading wire, .012 or .013
- **8** in. (20cm) 20-gauge half-hard wire
- **18** crimp beads
- **2** 25–35mm cones (Eclectica, 262-641-0910)
- box clasp (Jess Imports, 415-626-1433, jessimports.com)
- chainnose pliers
- roundnose pliers
- wire cutters
- crimping pliers (optional)

**earrings**
- **2** 8–10mm pearls
- **2** 5–6mm pearls
- **2** 6–10mm accent beads
- **1½** in. (3.8cm) chain, 4–5mm links
- **6** 1½-in. (3.8cm) head pins
- pair of decorative earring wires
- chainnose pliers
- roundnose pliers
- wire cutters

**1** earrings • On a head pin, string a small pearl. Make the first half of a wrapped loop. Repeat with an accent bead and a large pearl.

**2** Cut a three-link section of chain. Open the loop (Basics) of an earring wire. Attach the chain and close the loop.

**3** Attach one bead unit to each link and complete the wraps. Make a second earring to match the first.

# Moonstone ensemble

Some ancient civilizations believed that moonstone adornments made the wearer invisible, but this necklace-and-earring set will make you anything but. The simple pattern of crystals and rainbow moonstones celebrates June birthdays with an iridescence that won't be eclipsed.

**by Maria Camera**

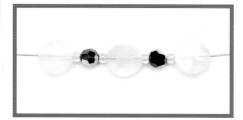

**1** necklace • Determine the finished length of your necklace. (This one is 17 in./43cm.) Add 6 in. (15cm) and cut a piece of beading wire to that length. On the wire, center a moonstone coin bead, an 11º seed bead, a round crystal, an 11º, a coin, an 11º, a round crystal, an 11º, and a coin.

**2** On each end, string an 11º, a bicone crystal, an 11º, a coin, an 11º, a round crystal, an 11º, and a coin. Repeat until the strand is within 1 in. (2.5cm) of the desired length.

**3** On one end, string an 11º, a round, an 11º, a crimp bead, an 11º, and a lobster claw clasp. Go back through the beads just strung and tighten the wire. Repeat on the other end, substituting a soldered jump ring or split ring for the clasp. Check the fit, and add or remove beads from each end if necessary. Crimp the crimp beads (see Basics, p. 8) and trim the excess wire.

**1** earrings • On a decorative head pin, string a moonstone coin bead, a spacer, a bicone crystal, an 11º seed bead, a round crystal, an 11º, a bicone, an 11º, a round crystal, and an 11º. Make a wrapped loop (Basics) above the top bead.

**2** Open the loop (Basics) of an earring wire and attach the dangle. Close the loop. Make a second earring to match the first.

## SupplyList

necklace
- 16-in. (41cm) strand 7mm faceted rainbow-moonstone coin beads
- **16–18** 4mm round crystals
- **14–16** 4mm bicone crystals
- 1g 11º seed beads
- flexible beading wire, .014 or .015
- **2** crimp beads
- lobster claw clasp and soldered jump ring or split ring
- chainnose or crimping pliers
- wire cutters
- split-ring pliers (optional)

earrings
- **2** 7mm faceted rainbow-moonstone coin beads
- **4** 4mm round crystals
- **4** 4mm bicone crystals
- **8** 11º seed beads
- **2** 4mm flat spacers
- **2** 2½-in. (6.4cm) decorative head pins
- pair of decorative earring wires
- chainnose pliers
- roundnose pliers
- wire cutters

# July

## Ruby

### Physical properties
Rubies are the hardest gemstone after diamonds and, in their purest, most desirable red form, are rarer than diamonds. In that clear, pure red state, rubies are also one of the most expensive gemstones. Often heat treated to improve their color and clarity, the stones range in color from orangey-red to nearly purple, with deep red being the most highly prized. Aside from the difference in color, there is no real distinction between rubies and sapphires – they are basically the same stone. Beads, cabochons, and nuggets can be found at affordable prices, but color and clarity vary. Rubies are usually panned from riverbeds, primarily in Southeast Asia and Eastern Africa.

### History and lore
Long prized by kings and emperors and set in crowns and insignia, rubies were thought in ancient times to receive their color from an inner fire and were associated with love, courage, and power. The name "ruby" comes from the Latin word *ruber* for red. Some say the stone ignites passions and inspires confidence; it also is a traditional symbol for love and success.

## Carnelian

### Physical properties
A member of the chalcedony family, carnelian varies in color from orange and white to reddish brown. The stone ranges from nearly transparent to nearly opaque. It is found all over the world and is fairly affordable when cut into beads and cabochons.

### History and lore
Ancient Egyptians believed that carnelian protected the wearer after death and often placed it on mummies to aid their passage to the afterlife. Romans thought the stone enhanced courage and strength, and modern healers think the stone is essential for restoring natural energy in the body. Many believe the stone increases creativity and courage and relieves anxiety.

# Rubies and pearls

Sumptuously simple to make, yet lavish in appearance, this necklace-and-earrings set combines the lustrous beauty of pearls with the glow and gleam of rubies. The rich red hues of the gemstones give this necklace a royal appeal.

**by Helene Tsigistras**

**1** **necklace** • Determine the finished length of your necklace. (This one is 17 in./43cm.) Add 6 in. (15cm), and cut a piece of flexible beading wire to that length. String a crimp bead and half of a clasp. Go back through the crimp bead. Crimp the crimp bead (see Basics, p. 8).

**2** String five pearls.

**3** String an 8mm accent bead, three pearls, a briolette, and three pearls. Repeat until the necklace is within 2 in. (5cm) of the desired length.

**4** String an 8mm, five pearls, a crimp bead, and the other half of the clasp. Go back through the crimp bead, and crimp the crimp bead. Trim the excess wire.

**1** **earrings** • Cut a 6-in. (15cm) piece of wire. String a briolette two inches from one end of the wire and make a set of wraps (Basics) above the bead with the short tail. Trim the short tail.

**2** String an 8mm accent bead on the wire, and make a wrapped loop above it.

Open the loop (Basics) of an earring finding and attach the earring. Make a second earring to match the first.

## SupplyList

**necklace**
- **8** 12 x 15mm flat briolettes, ruby crystal
- **9** 8mm accent beads
- 16-in. strand 5mm freshwater pearls
- flexible beading wire, .012–.015
- **2** crimp beads
- hook-and-eye clasp
- crimping pliers
- wire cutters

**earrings**
- **2** 12 x 15mm flat briolettes, ruby crystal
- **2** 8mm accent beads
- 12 in. (30cm) 24-gauge half-hard wire
- pair of earring findings
- chainnose pliers
- roundnose pliers
- wire cutters

### EDITOR'S TIP
The accent beads in this necklace feature crystals that pick up the ruby tones of the briolettes. They were purchased at Eclectica (262-641-0910). You can also use Swarovski rhinestone rounds or 8mm filigree or marcasite beads for a similar effect.

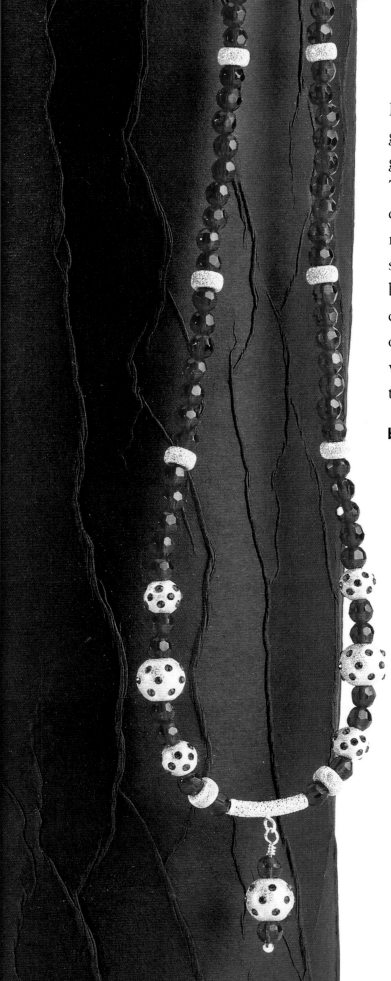

# Necklace in ruby red

Red-dyed quartz is a great substitute for genuine rubies. Though it's rich in color, its cost is reasonable. Mix in a sprinkle of stardust beads with ruby crystal accents for dazzling results that will lend a little glitz to any wardrobe.

**by Paulette Biedenbender**

**1** Determine the finished length of your necklace. (This one is 18 in./46cm.) Add 6 in. (15cm) and cut a piece of beading wire to that length. Center the tube bead on the wire.

**2** To make the pendant, string a 4mm round, an 8mm silver, and a 4mm round on a decorative head pin. Make the first half of a wrapped loop (see Basics, p. 8) above the bead.

**3** Attach the pendant's loop to the tube bead's loop and complete the wraps.

**4** On each side of the tube, string a 4mm round, a rondelle, a 4mm round, a 6mm silver, two 4mm rounds, 8mm silver, two 4mm rounds, and a 6mm silver.

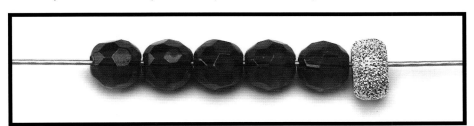

**5** On each end, string five 4mm rounds and a rondelle. Repeat three more times on each end, adding two 4mm rounds to each consecutive pattern.

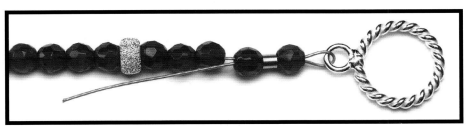

**6** On each end, string 4mm rounds until the necklace is within 1 in. (2.5cm) of the desired length. String a crimp bead, a 4mm round, and half of a clasp. Go back through the last three beads strung and tighten the wire. Check the fit, and add or remove an equal number of beads from each end if necessary. Crimp the crimp beads (Basics) and trim the excess wire.

## SupplyList

- 16-in. (41cm) strand 4mm round faceted red-dyed quartz
- **10** 5mm rondelles, stardust finish
- **3** 8mm silver and faceted crystal birthstone accent beads, ruby
- **4** 6mm silver and faceted crystal birthstone accent beads, ruby
- 9 x 2mm curved tube bead with loop, stardust finish
- 2-in. (5cm) decorative head pin
- flexible beading wire, .014 or .015
- **2** crimp beads
- toggle clasp
- chainnose pliers
- roundnose pliers
- wire cutters
- crimping pliers (optional)

# Carnelian earrings

These fiery carnelian earrings are perfect for adding a little spice to any wardrobe. The bright colors and movement of the fringe are sure to get some attention.

**by Paulette Biedenbender**

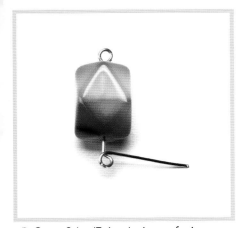

**1** Cut a 3-in. (7.6cm) piece of wire. Make a plain loop (see Basics, p. 8) at one end and string on a nugget. Make the first half of a wrapped loop (Basics) below the nugget.

**2** Cut one piece of chain with seven links (1¾ in./4.4cm) and one with five links (1¼ in./3.2cm). If using the long-and-short style of chain, as shown here, leave a short link on one end of each chain and a long link at the other end. Slide the short-link ends onto the loop below the nugget. Complete the wraps.

# Supply List

- **2** 11 x 14mm faceted carnelian nuggets
- **24** 6mm oval carnelian beads
- **1g** size 11º seed beads, complementary color
- **6 in.** (15.2cm) long-and-short diamond chain, 3.5mm, gold filled
- **24** 1½-in. (3.8cm) 22-gauge head pins, gold filled
- **6 in.** (15.2cm) 22-gauge wire, gold filled
- pair of earring wires
- chainnose pliers
- roundnose pliers
- wire cutters

**3** To make the dangles, string a seed bead, an oval bead, and a seed bead on a head pin. Make the first half of a wrapped loop above the bead. Make a total of 12 dangles.

**4** Attach a dangle to the bottom link of the long chain. Complete the wraps. Continue attaching dangles, alternating from the left side of one long link to the right side of the next long link. Continue this pattern until you have attached seven dangles.

Repeat steps 4 through 6 on the shorter chain, attaching five dangles.

**5** Open the loop (Basics) of an earring wire and string it through the loop above the carnelian nugget. Close the loop. Make a second earring to match the first.

# August

## Peridot

### Physical properties

Peridot is a light, transparent green stone that ranges in hue from bright chartreuse to olive green. The intense color has become more popular over recent years, and the stone is widely available and fairly affordable. Peridot beads, cabochons, and pendants are easy to find. Often, peridot is treated with oil or resin to improve its appearance.

### History and lore

Peridot's popularity has risen and fallen throughout the ages. Many famous emeralds, such as those owned by Cleopatra, were probably peridot, but only in recent years has the stone's popularity surged. The beautiful green color inspired the legend that the stone was a gift from the gods to celebrate spring. It's believed to be a good luck stone, and thought to bring its wearer success and peace.

## Sardonyx

### Physical properties

Sardonyx is a banded agate gemstone that ranges in color from orange and white to gray and white. Sometimes dyed to enhance their color, the stones can be rich or subtly shaded. The lines of the banding tend to be very regular and straight, and no two stones are exactly alike. Sardonyx is widely available in a variety of forms, including beads and cabochons.

### History and lore

Sardonyx was popular and widely used in ancient Roman and Egyptian cultures and in Elizabethan times. The banding makes the stone perfect for carving cameos and intaglios, and bullseye banding patterns are considered especially valuable in beads and cabochons. The stone is said to increase the eloquence of public speakers and give the wearer powerful charisma. Healers sometimes use sardonyx to treat insect bites and stings.

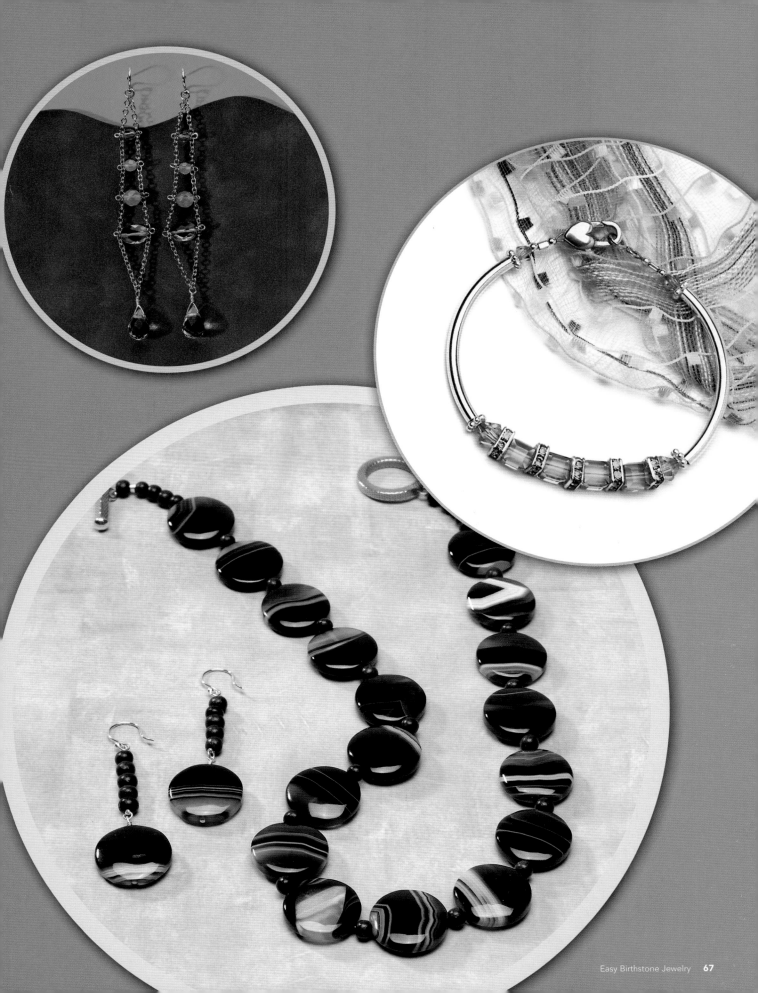

# Slinky peridot earrings

Delicate chain showcases
beautiful green peridot
in varying shades. The
length of these dangles
is eye-catching, yet the
earrings are casual
enough for everyday
wear. These earrings are
a great way to use leftover
beads of any hue.

**by Jane Konkel**

**1** Cut two 2½-in. (6.4cm) pieces of chain. Open a jump ring (see Basics, p. 8) and attach each chain's end. Close the jump ring.

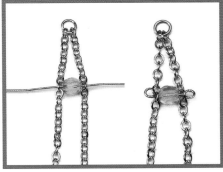

**2** Cut a 1½-in. (3.8cm) piece of wire. String a 4mm round crystal on the wire. String the ninth link of each chain on each side of the bead. Make a plain loop (Basics) on each end.

**3** Repeat step 2 with the 5mm round on the 16th links; the 7mm round on the 23rd links; and the 7 x 10mm rectangle on the 31st links.

**4** Cut a 2-in. (5cm) piece of wire. String a top-drilled briolette and complete the wraps above the bead (Basics). Make the first half of a wrapped loop (Basics) above the wraps.

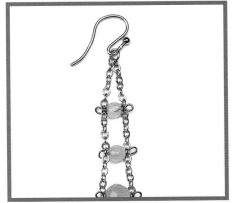

**5** Attach the ends of both chains to the briolette dangle. Complete the wraps.

**6** Open an earring wire and attach the chain dangle. Close the wire. Make a second earring to match the first.

## SupplyList

- **2** 9 x 12mm peridot top-drilled briolettes
- **2** 7 x 10mm faceted peridot rectangles
- **2** 7mm round crystals
- **2** 5mm round crystals
- **2** 4mm Czech fire-polished round crystals
- 10½ in. (26.7cm) gold-filled cable chain, 1mm links
- 16 in. (41cm) 24-gauge gold-filled half-hard wire
- **2** 4mm jump rings
- pair of earring wires
- chainnose pliers
- roundnose pliers
- wire cutters

**EDITOR'S TIP**
Lightly mark the ninth, 16th, 23rd, and 31st links of each of the 2½-in. (6.4cm) chains with a water-soluble marker. The links will be more visible, making it easier to string the wire through the corresponding links. When the earrings are finished, the marks will be covered by beads.

# Pretty peridot set

Peridot crystals get extra sparkle from matching squaredelles in this easy-to-make set. You can make both the bracelet and the earrings in less than half an hour — leaving you plenty of time to show off your style.

**by Patricia Bartlein**

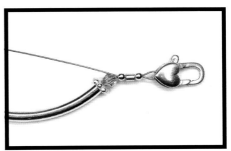

**1** bracelet • Determine the finished length of your bracelet, add 5 in. (13cm), and cut a piece of beading wire to that length. On the wire, center an alternating pattern of five squaredelles and four cube crystals.

**2** On each end of the wire, string a 6mm bicone crystal, a flat spacer, a curved tube bead, a flat spacer, and a 4mm bicone crystal.

**3** On one end, string a round spacer, a crimp bead, a round spacer, and a lobster claw clasp. Go back through the beads just strung and tighten the wire. Repeat on the other end, substituting a soldered jump ring for the clasp. Check the fit, and add or remove beads from each end if necessary. Crimp the crimp beads (see Basics, p. 8) and trim the excess wire.

**1** earrings • On a head pin, string a cube crystal, a squaredelle, and a bicone crystal. Make the first half of a wrapped loop (Basics).

**2** Attach the dangle to the loop of an earring post. Complete the wraps. Make a second earring to match the first.

## Supply List

### bracelet
- 2 40mm silver curved tube beads
- 5 6mm peridot squaredelles
- 4 6mm cube crystals
- 2 6mm peridot bicone crystals
- 2 4mm peridot bicone crystals
- 4 5mm flat spacers
- 4 3mm round spacers
- flexible beading wire, .014 or .015
- 2 crimp beads
- lobster claw clasp and soldered jump ring
- chainnose or crimping pliers
- wire cutters

### earrings
- 2 6mm peridot squaredelles
- 2 6mm cube crystals
- 2 6mm peridot bicone crystals
- 2 2-in. (5cm) head pins
- pair of earring posts with ear nuts
- chainnose pliers
- roundnose pliers
- wire cutters

# Sardonyx circles

The parallel bands and dramatic geometrics of these earth-toned sardonyx beads are a perfect match for organic wood accent beads. Subtle yet sophisticated, this necklace is an excellent choice for everyday style.

**by Helene Tsigistras**

**1** necklace • Determine the finished length of your necklace. (This one is 18 in./46cm.) Add 6 in. (15cm), and cut a piece of flexible beading wire to that length. String a crimp bead a wood bead, and half of a clasp. Go back through the beads just strung, tighten the wire, and crimp the crimp bead (see Basics, p. 8). Trim the excess wire.

**2** String three wood beads and a sardonyx disk. Continue stringing, alternating wood beads and sardonyx disks until you are within 3 in. of the desired finished length. End with a disk. String three wood beads, a crimp bead, a wood bead, and the other clasp half. Go back through the last wood bead and the crimp, and crimp the crimp bead. Trim the excess wire.

**1** earrings • String a sardonyx disk on a head pin and make a wrapped loop (Basics) above the bead.

**2** Make the first half of a wrapped loop at the end of a 3 in. (7.6cm) piece of wire. Attach the sardonyx unit and complete the wraps.

**3** String five wood beads on the wire and make a wrapped loop above the beads.

Open the loop (Basics) of an earring finding and attach the earring. Close the loop. Make a second earring to match the first.

# Supply List

**necklace**
- **17** 20mm sardonyx disks
- **24** 5mm wood beads
- flexible beading wire, .012–.015
- **2** crimp beads
- toggle clasp
- crimping pliers
- wire cutters

**earrings**
- **2** 20mm sardonyx disks
- **10** 5mm wood beads
- 6 in. (15cm) 24-gauge half-hard wire
- **2** 24-gauge head pins
- pair of earring findings
- chainnose pliers
- roundnose pliers
- wire cutters

# September

## Sapphire

### Physical properties

Sapphires are one of the hardest gemstones after diamonds, and belong to the same family as rubies. Best known in their brilliant royal blue shade, sapphires in fact come in a wide range of colors, including greens, yellows, and violets. Sapphires are mined from riverbeds worldwide, but large stones are rare. Because of their high value, transparent sapphires are more often found as cut gems, but stones with inclusions can be found as beads.

### History and lore

Sapphires enjoy worldwide popularity and have long symbolized truth and been an emblem for mystics, saints, and other religious figures. Said to encourage faithfulness, they often are symbols of love and commitment, making them popular for engagement rings and anniversary jewelry. The stone's blue tones are supposed to soothe and calm the wearer, dispelling unwanted thoughts.

## Lapis lazuli

### Physical properties

The rich blue color and sparkling golden flecks of lapis lazuli come from several minerals combined together with flecks or veins of pyrite (or "fool's gold"). Lapis lazuli is found throughout the world, with the best specimens traditionally from Afghanistan. The stone is not especially hard, so it is easily made into beads, cabochons, carvings, and more.

### History and lore

Highly prized by ancient Mesopotamians, Egyptians, Persians, Greeks, and Romans, lapis lazuli was used to decorate King Tutankhamen's tomb in Egypt and ground up and used in paint during the Middle Ages and Renaissance. Lapis lazuli is considered a very spiritual stone, used to absorb spiritual energy and promote the link between the physical and metaphysical worlds. Some believe it wards off evil and protects truth.

# Edgy sapphire dangles

Sapphire crystals punctuate free-form draped chain in this dramatic bracelet and earrings. A mix of light and dark crystals accents grays and blues well, while a bracelet and earrings in gold provide an exotic look with high contrast.

## by Brenda Schweder

**1** **bracelet** • String a crystal on a head pin. Make a plain loop (see Basics, p. 8). Make 15 to 20 crystal units using 3mm and 5 or 6mm bicones and 4mm cubes.

**2** Cut a 12–18-in. (30–46cm) piece of figaro chain. Open a jump ring (Basics) and attach an end link of chain and a loop of a bracelet. Close the jump ring.

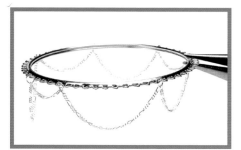

**3** Use jump rings to attach the chain to the bracelet's loops, draping the chain as desired. When you reach the jump ring from step 2, open it and attach the end link. Close the jump ring.

**4** Repeat steps 2 and 3 with a piece of cable chain.

**5** Open the loop of a crystal unit. Attach it to a chain link or to a loop of the bracelet. Close the loop. Attach the remaining crystal units as desired.

**EDITOR'S TIP**
Drape chain as desired for two different earrings, or follow the instructions for an easy way to make a matching pair.

**1** earrings • On a head pin, string a crystal. Make a plain loop. Make 16 to 22 crystal units using 3mm and 5 or 6mm bicones and 4mm cubes.

# Supply List

## bracelet
- **4–6** 5mm or 6mm bicone crystals
- **4–6** 3mm bicone crystals
- **7–8** 4mm cube crystals
- 3-in. (7.6cm) bangle bracelet with ruffled loop edges
- 12–18 in. (30–46cm) cable chain, 3–4mm links
- 12–18 in. (30–46cm) figaro chain, 3–4mm links
- **15–20** 1-in. (2.5cm) head pins
- **10–15** 3–4mm inside diameter jump rings
- chainnose pliers
- roundnose pliers
- wire cutters

## earrings
- **4–6** 5mm or 6mm bicone crystals
- **4–6** 3mm bicone crystals
- **8–10** 4mm cube crystals
- 14–16 in. (36–41cm) cable chain, 3–4mm links
- 9–11 in. (23–28cm) figaro chain, 3–4mm links
- **16–22** 1-in. (2.5cm) head pins
- **16–20** 3–4mm inside diameter jump rings
- pair of hoop earrings with loops
- chainnose pliers
- roundnose pliers
- wire cutters

**2** Cut a 4–5-in. (10–13cm) piece of figaro chain. Open a jump ring and attach an end link of chain and the loop of a hoop earring. Close the jump ring. Use a jump ring to attach the other end link.

**3** Use a jump ring to attach the chain to the earring, draping the chain as desired. Repeat steps 2 and 3 with the second hoop earring.

**4** Cut a 7–8-in. (18–20cm) piece of cable chain. Use jump rings to connect the chain to one of the earrings as desired. Repeat with the second hoop earring.

**5** Open the loop of a crystal unit. Attach it to a chain link or to an earring loop. Close the loop. Attach the remaining crystal units to each earring as desired.

# Silk and sapphires

Sparkling sapphire-blue crystals spill from an art-glass pendant and twine through sky-hued silk ribbons in this dreamy necklace-and-earrings set. Easy chain dangles add movement and sparkle for a look that's as appealing as blue skies and calm seas.

**by Helene Tsigistras**

**1** **necklace •** Cut four pieces of chain to the following lengths: ¾ in. (1.9cm), 1 in. (2.5cm), 1¼ in. (3.2cm), and 1½ in. (3.8cm). String a bicone crystal on a head pin and make the first half of a wrapped loop (see Basics, p. 8). Attach the end link of any one of the lengths of chain and complete the wraps. Repeat with a second and third bicone, and with an oval crystal.

**2** Cut three 4-in. (10cm) lengths of 22-gauge wire, and set two aside. On the remaining wire, make the first half of a wrapped loop and attach the top link of each chain. Complete the wraps. String the glass shell bead over the wrapped loop.

**3** Make a wrapped loop above the shell bead, taking care to make the loop large enough to fit over two silk ribbons.

**4** Determine the finished length of your necklace. (This one is 21 in./53cm.) Add 6 in. (15cm), and cut one strand of flexible beading wire to that length. Center the pendant on the flexible beading wire. On each side of the necklace, string a bicone, an oval, and a bicone, and 22 cylinder beads. Repeat on each end until the strand is within 2½ in. (6.4cm) of the desired finished length, ending with cylinder beads.

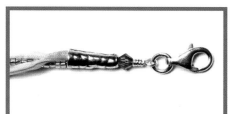

**5** Thread two silk ribbons through the pendant loop and center the necklace on the ribbons. Each side should have two ribbons and a beaded strand.

Make a wrapped loop on one end of each of the remaining 4-in. wires. String a crimp bead and a wrapped loop on each end of the beaded strand. Go back through the crimp bead. Thread each of the ribbons through the corresponding wrapped loop and tie the ribbons around the loop with tight overhand knots (Basics). Check the fit; add or remove cylinder beads from the beaded strand as necessary. Crimp the crimp beads (Basics) and trim the excess wire. Trim the ribbon near the knot.

**6** String a silver cone and a bicone over each wrapped loop. Make a wrapped loop above each cone. Open a jump ring (Basics) and attach a lobster-claw clasp to one end of the necklace. Close the jump ring. Use a jump ring to attach a soldered or split ring to the other end of the necklace.

## Supply List

**necklace**
- 35mm art glass bead, shell or cone-shaped
- **11** 5x10mm oval crystals, sapphire
- **25** 4mm bicone crystals
- 3g 11º Japanese cylinder beads, blue-gray luster
- **2** 4x12mm cones
- flexible beading wire, .012 –.015
- **2** silk ribbons, sky blue
- 12-in. (30cm) 22-gauge half-hard wire
- 5 in. (13cm) decorative chain
- **4** 1½-in. (3.8cm) head pins
- **2** crimp beads
- lobster-claw clasp and soldered jump ring
- chainnose pliers
- roundnose pliers
- crimping pliers
- wire cutters

**earrings**
- **2** 5x10mm oval crystals, sapphire
- **6** 4mm bicone crystals
- **2** 4x12mm cones
- 8 in. (30cm) 22-gauge half-hard wire
- 10 in. (25cm) decorative chain
- **8** 1½-in. (3.8cm) head pins
- pair of earring findings
- chainnose pliers
- roundnose pliers
- wire cutters

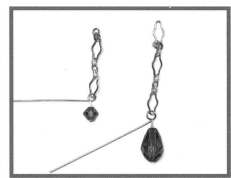

**1** earrings • Cut four pieces of chain to the following lengths: ¾ in. (1.9cm), 1 in. (2.5cm), 1¼ in. (3.2cm), and 1½ in. (3.8cm). String a bicone crystal on a head pin and make the first half of a wrapped loop. Repeat twice, and make a fourth headpin unit with an oval crystal. Attach each of the loops to the end link of a piece of chain and complete the wraps.

**2** On a 2 in. (5cm) piece of wire, make the first half of a wrapped loop, attach the four chain units, and finish the wraps.

**3** String a cone over the wrapped loop. String a bicone above the cone and make a wrapped loop. Open the loop on an earring finding and attach the earring. Close the loop. Make a second earring to match the first.

# Lapis lazuli necklace

Highlight lapis beads with curved silver findings in a necklace that moves from two strands to one and back again. If you'd like to add more contrast to the design, gold findings would act as a dramatic foil.

**by Paulette Biedenbender**

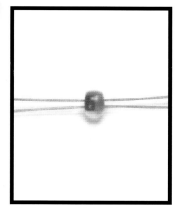

**1** Cut two 30-in. (76cm) lengths of Fireline and center a seed bead on the two strands.

**2** Bring all four ends together and string a button-shaped lapis, a round lapis, a diamond-shaped lapis, another round, a 3mm silver bead, a curved tube bead, and another 3mm.

**3** Separate the four strands into two pairs. String a 3mm silver bead onto each of the pairs.

**4** String a curved tube bead, a 3mm, a round lapis, a diamond-shaped lapis, a round lapis, and a 3mm on each end of the necklace.

**5** Separate the two strands of one pair and string a 3mm on each. On the outer strand, string a button-shaped lapis, a round lapis, and a button-shaped lapis. On the inner strand, string a round, a button, and a round. String the two-strand bead with the lower end on the outer side of the necklace. On the outer strand, string a round lapis, a button, a round, and 3mm. On the inner strand, string a button, a round lapis, a button, and 3mm.

**6** String a 3mm, a round lapis, a diamond-shaped lapis, a round, and a 3mm over both strands. Repeat steps 5-6 on the other end of the necklace.

Repeat the two patterns until the necklace sides are approximately 7 in. (18cm) or the desired length. Allow at least 3 in. (7.6cm) for finishing.

**7** To attach the clasp, string a 3mm, a round lapis, a 3mm, and a bead tip over both strands. Separate the strands and string a seed bead on one of them. Tie a surgeon's knot over the bead (see Basics, p. 8), tightening the knot as you slide the bead into the bead tip.

Glue the knot. When the glue is dry, closely trim the excess Fireline and close the bead tip with chainnose pliers. Repeat on the other end of the necklace.

## SupplyList

- 16-in. (41cm) strand 12mm diamond-shaped lapis lazuli
- 16-in. strand 4mm round lapis
- 16-in. strand 4mm button-shaped lapis
- **6** 13.4mm two-strand beads
- **3** 13mm curved tube beads
- **44** 3mm round silver beads
- Fireline fishing line, 6 lb. test
- **3** seed beads
- **2** bead tips
- G-S Hypo Cement
- chainnose pliers

# October

## Opal

### Physical properties

Opals come in a wide range of colors, but it is the iridescence and color play within the stones that make them special. Australia is the largest source for the gem, while Mexico provides the red, orange, and yellow fire opal variety. Opals are composed of two to six percent water, which means they'll become brittle if they dry out. For this reason, opals love to be worn frequently and cleaned with care. Be sure to ask a jeweler about the best way to care for your opals if they have undergone any treatments to protect the stone or enhance the color. If you like the iridescence of opals without the expense and care, synthetic opals and crystal alternatives are easy to find.

### History and lore

Australian Aborginal legend says opals were created when the storm god shattered a rainbow. Some ancient cultures thought opals could turn the wearer invisible. Opals are held in high regard because of the mystery of their changing colors, and some healers believe they help improve eyesight. They supposedly also enhance foresight and intuition.

## Pink Tourmaline

### Physical properties

Tourmaline is available in a wide range of colors and shades – in fact, its variable colors are part of what makes it so special – but the pink variety in particular is noted as October's birthstone. The stone can range from transparent to translucent with milky inclusions, and it is fairly hard, so it comes in a range of shapes including beads, cabochons, and carvings.

### History and lore

Pink tourmaline is thought to help one let go of the past, and when worn it is believed to attract compassion and love. It transforms negative thoughts and actions into positive responses, and some believe it to be particularly helpful for women.

# Luxurious opal necklace

If you're captivated by the fiery colors that dance inside opals, but concerned about their need for delicate handling, synthetic opals may be the perfect compromise. Add blue Venetian foil-lined beads to accentuate the hue that the faux opals cast. An opal-accented clasp works the authentic stone into the final piece.

**by Linda Augsburg**

**1** Determine the finished length of your necklace. (This one is 18 in./46cm.) Add 8 in. (20cm), and cut a piece of beading wire to that length.

Center a seed bead on the wire. Fold the wire in half and thread both ends through one diamond-shaped bead.

**2** String four seed beads and a triangle-shaped bead on each wire as shown.

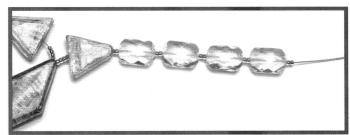

**3** Working on one end at a time, string an alternating pattern of two seed beads and an opal bead four times. End with two seed beads. Repeat on the opposite end.

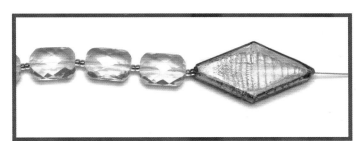

**4** String a diamond-shaped bead on each end.

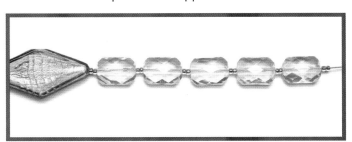

**5** Repeat step 3, stringing five opal beads instead of four. End with two seed beads.

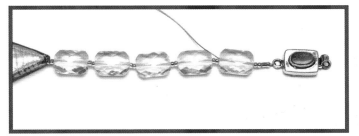

**6** String a crimp bead, a seed bead, and one half of a clasp on one end. Check the fit, and add or remove beads from each end, if necessary. Go back through the beads just strung, tighten the wire and crimp the crimp bead (see Basics, p. 8). Trim the excess wire. Repeat on the other end.

# Opal drop strand

A strand of blue opal briolettes requires little embellishment to look striking. String a few tiny bronze faceted seed beads to space the briolettes and accent their brown tones. Or, try silver-colored seed beads for a more modern look.

**by Naomi Fujimoto**

**1** Determine the finished length of your necklace. (This one is 15 in./38cm.) Add 6 in. (15cm), and cut a piece of beading wire to that length. Center a briolette on the wire. (If you're using briolettes in graduated sizes, string the largest briolette.)

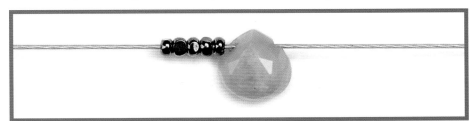

**2** On each end, string five 13º seed beads and a briolette. Repeat until the strand is within 1 in. (2.5cm) of the desired length.

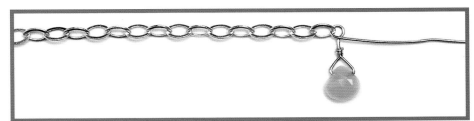

**3** Cut a 3-in. (7.6cm) piece of 26-gauge wire. String a briolette and make a set of wraps above it (see Basics, p. 8). Make the first half of a wrapped loop (Basics) above the wraps.

Cut a 2-in. (5cm) piece of chain. Attach the dangle to one end and complete the wraps.

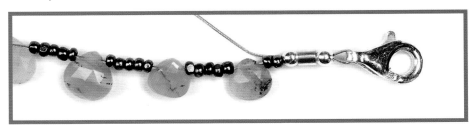

**4** On one end of the necklace, string a spacer, a crimp bead, a spacer, and a lobster claw clasp. Repeat on the other end, substituting the chain extender for the clasp. Check the fit, and add or remove beads from each end, if necessary. Go back through the beads just strung, tighten the wire, and crimp the crimp beads (Basics). Trim the excess wire.

## SupplyList

- **40–50** 5–7mm blue opal briolettes
- hank 13º seed beads (Charlottes)
- **4** 2mm round spacers
- flexible beading wire, .012 or .013
- 3 in. (7.6cm) 26-gauge half-hard wire
- 2 in. (5cm) chain, 3–4mm links
- **2** crimp beads
- lobster claw clasp
- chainnose pliers
- roundnose pliers
- wire cutters
- crimping pliers (optional)

### EDITOR'S TIP
Size 13º Charlottes are usually sold in hanks of 12-in. (30cm) strands. You'll need only one strand for this necklace.

# Charming pink tourmaline

This bracelet is filled with a fringe of dangles in all shades of pink that dance along your wrist with every movement. Adding charms allows you to personalize the bracelet for yourself or someone else.

**by Helene Tsigistras**

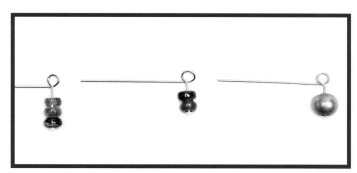

**1** String three 4mms on a head pin, and make the first half of a wrapped loop (see Basics, p. 8). Make 56 three-bead units. String two 4mm tourmaline beads on a head pin, and make the first half of a wrapped loop. Make 56 two-bead units. String a pearl on a head pin, and make the first half of a wrapped loop. Make 28 pearl units.

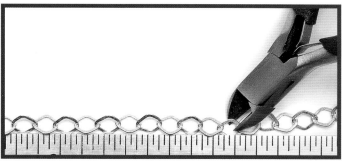

**2** Determine the finished length of your bracelet, subtract the length of a clasp, and cut a piece of chain to that length.

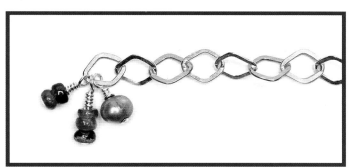

**3** Start at one end of the chain and attach three dangles to the first link. Continue down the chain, adding three to six dangles to each link. (On this bracelet a pearl dangle, two two-bead dangles, and two three-bead dangles were attached to most links.)

**4** If you wish to add a charm, open a jump ring (Basics), attach the charm to a link of the chain, and close the jump ring. Add additional charms the same way.

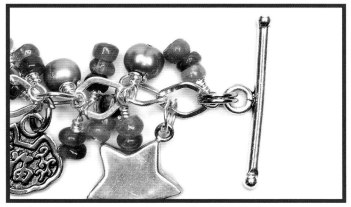

**5** Open a split ring (Basics). Use the split ring to attach one half of a clasp to one end of the bracelet. Attach the other half of the clasp to the other end with another split ring.

## SupplyList

- 16-in. (41cm) strand 4mm pink tourmaline rondelles
- **28** 5mm pearls, pink
- silver charms (optional)
- 6–8 in. (15–20cm) 5–8mm cable chain
- **2** split rings
- jump rings to attach charms
- **140 or more** 24-gauge head pins
- toggle clasp
- chainnose pliers
- roundnose pliers
- split ring pliers (optional)
- wire cutters

# November

## Topaz

### Physical properties
While topaz can be found in a range of colors, the traditional shade ranges from gold to taupe. It is a hard, transparent stone, more frequently cut into a faceted, set gem than into beads. High water content in the stone is responsible for the color, which is sometimes improved through heat treatments. Topaz is found worldwide, usually alongside granite in riverbeds.

### History and lore
Ancient Greeks believed topaz could make its wearer invisible, and during the Middle Ages it was used to detect poison. Believed to be a powerful healing stone during certain phases of the moon, topaz was thought particularly effective for providing relief from asthma and insomnia and improving circulation. Also associated with honor and power, topaz is supposed to bring balance and wealth to the wearer.

## Lemon Quartz

### Physical properties
Lemon quartz is a variety of quartz similar to citrine (another November birthstone) and amethyst, but with a distinctive lemon-yellow color. The stone comes primarily from Brazil and is made by heat treating yellow quartz or amethyst to get a strong yellow shade. The clarity ranges from transparent to translucent and the gem is available in a variety of sizes and shapes.

### History and lore
According to lore, lemon quartz affords protection from snake bites, eliminates negative thoughts, and relieves anxiety and depression. Some believe it also helps wearers organize and clarify their lives, allowing them to focus their energy on the positive.

# Set of twinkling topaz

Highlight the beauty of topaz with three simple jewelry pieces. The delicate necklace boasts a single pendant, while the bracelet is resplendent with nugget-sized crystals. Add easy chain earrings to extend the golden glow.

**by Irina Miech**

**1** necklace • Cut a piece of chain 1 in. (2.5cm) shorter than the desired length of your necklace. (This necklace is 16 in./41cm.) On a head pin, string a crystal and a spacer. Make the first half of a wrapped loop (see Basics, p. 8).

**2** Attach the dangle to the chain's center link and complete the wraps. Check the fit, allowing 1 in. (2.5cm) for finishing. Trim chain from each end, if necessary.

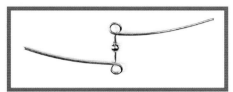

**3** Cut a 3-in. (7.6cm) piece of wire. Make the first half of a wrapped loop. String a spacer and make the first half of a wrapped loop on the other end. Repeat to make two spacer units.

**4** Attach the loop of one spacer unit to one end of the chain. Attach a lobster claw clasp to the other loop of the spacer unit. Complete the wraps. Repeat on the other end, substituting a soldered jump ring for the clasp.

**1** bracelet • Determined the finished length of your bracelet, add 5 in. (13cm) and cut a piece of beading wire to that length. String a 12mm crystal, a spacer, a 16mm crystal, and a spacer. Repeat until the bracelet is within 1 in. (2.5cm) of the desired length, ending with a crystal.

**2** On one end, string a spacer, a crimp bead, a spacer, and a lobster claw clasp. Repeat on the other end, substituting a soldered jump ring for the clasp. Check the fit, and add or remove beads if necessary. Go back through the last few beads strung, tighten the wires, and crimp the crimp beads (Basics). Trim the excess wire.

**1** earrings • On a head pin, string a crystal and a spacer. Make the first half of a wrapped loop.

**2** Cut a ½-in. (1.3cm) piece of chain. Attach the loop to one end of the chain and complete the wraps.

**3** Open the loop (Basics) of an earring wire and attach the dangle. Close the loop. Make a second earring to match the first.

## SupplyList

**necklace**
- 16mm topaz crystal
- **3** 2mm round spacers
- 6 in. (15cm) 24-gauge half-hard wire
- 15–18 in. (38–46cm) rolo chain, 2–3mm links
- 2-in. (5cm) 22-gauge head pin
- lobster claw clasp and soldered jump ring
- chainnose pliers
- roundnose pliers
- wire cutters

**bracelet**
- **5–6** 16mm topaz crystals
- **5–7** 12mm topaz crystals
- **14–16** 3mm round spacers
- flexible beading wire, .014 or .015
- **2** crimp beads
- lobster claw clasp and soldered jump ring
- chainnose or crimping pliers
- wire cutters

**earrings**
- **2** 12mm topaz crystals
- **2** 2mm round spacers
- 1 in. (2.5cm) rolo chain, 2–3mm links
- **2** 2-in. (5cm) 22-gauge head pins
- pair of earring wires
- chainnose pliers
- roundnose pliers
- wire cutters

**SUPPLY TIP**
For these projects, use Swarovski crystals in style #5523. The dark color is crystal copper; the light color is crystal golden shadow.

# Layered topaz necklace

This long, slinky necklace boasts four layers of topaz beads on fine gold mesh wire. Tiny, nearly invisible knots anchor the beads in place and are a breeze to make.

**by Helene Tsigistras**

**1** Determine the finished length of the shortest strand of your necklace. (The shortest strand of this necklace is 20 in./51cm). Add 4 in. (10cm) and cut a piece of wire mesh to that length. Add 8 in. (20cm) and cut a second piece of mesh to that length. Add 12 in. (30cm) and cut a third piece to that length. Add 20 in. (51cm) and cut a piece of beading wire to that length. (The longest strand in this necklace is 34 in./86cm).

Center an oval, a rondelle, an oval, a rondelle, an oval, a rondelle, and an oval on the shortest piece of mesh wire.

**2** Tie an overhand knot (see Basics, p. 8) 2½ in. (6.4cm) from the centered cluster. You can use an awl or needle to position the knot. Repeat on the other end. String a bicone on each end and tie an overhand knot next to each bicone.

**3** Center a rondelle on the second strand of wire mesh and tie an overhand knot on each side. Measure 2½ in. from the rondelles, and tie an overhand knot on each end. String an oval on each end and tie an overhand knot after each bead. Measure 2½ in. from the ovals and tie another overhand knot on each end. String a rondelle on each end and tie another overhand knot after each bead. Repeat measuring from the rondelles and knotting, this time adding an oval to each end of the strand.

**4a** Center an oval bead on the third strand of wire mesh, and tie an overhand knot on either side of the bead.

**b** On each end, measure 2 in. (5cm) from the oval. Tie an overhand knot. On each end, string: oval, bicone, rondelle, bicone, and oval. Tie an overhand knot.

**c** Measure 3 in. (7.6cm) and string another five-bead set on each end of the necklace. Tie an overhand knot after the last bead on each end.

**5a** On the last strand, center a bicone, a rondelle, and a bicone, and tie overhand knots next to the beads.

**b** On each end, measure 4 in. (10cm), tie an overhand knot, string an oval, and tie another overhand knot.

**c** Repeat **a** and **b** twice on each side, alternating three-bead clusters and oval beads.

## SupplyList

- **21** 9x6mm topaz oval crystals
- **16** 6mm topaz bicone crystals
- **13** 8mm topaz rondelle crystals
- mesh wire ribbon
- **2** pinch ends
- spring clasp
- split ring
- awl or needle, optional
- chainnose pliers
- wire cutters
- E6000 adhesive

**6** Gather together the four strands and check the fit of the necklace, allowing 1 in. (2.5cm) for finishing. Trim the excess wire mesh from each side, leaving about ¼ in. (6mm) extra length on each side. Fold the ends in by ¼ in., wrap the strands together, and glue the ends.

**7** Close a pinch end clasp over the glued ends with chainnose pliers. Use wire cutters to trim away any excess mesh.

**8** Open the loop or jump ring (Basics) for a spring clasp and attach it to one pinch end. Attach a split ring to the other pinch end.

### EDITOR'S TIP
Twist and compress the very end of the mesh until it slides easily through the beads.

# Long, lean lemon quartz

**by Naomi Fujimoto**

Take the long view with a skinny necklace that dips down to your navel. This version substitutes faceted lemon quartz for traditional topaz. Unfettered by a clasp, 42 inches of gold chain unite the beads. Loop the necklace around a second time for a more conservative look.

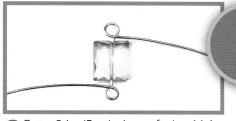

**1** necklace • Determine the finished length of your necklace. Divide that measurement by 2.25 and cut that number pieces of 1¾-in. (4.4cm) chain. (This necklace is 42½ in./1.1m, with a total of 19 bead units and 19 pieces of chain.) If you want a bead unit to fall in the center of the necklace, cut an odd number of chains segments.

**2** Cut a 2-in. (5cm) piece of wire. Make the first half of a wrapped loop (see Basics, p. 8) on one end. String a 6mm bead and make the first half of a wrapped loop on the other end. Make one bead unit for each piece of chain.

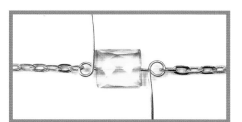

**3** Attach a chain to each loop on one bead unit. Complete the wraps.

**4** Continue attaching bead units and chains until the necklace is the desired length. End with a chain. Check the fit. If necessary, add or remove a bead unit or a chain, or trim an equal amount of chain from each end.

**5** Attach the loop on a bead unit to each chain end. Complete the wraps.

**1** earrings • String a 6mm bead on a head pin and make a plain loop (Basics) above the bead. Cut a 2-in. (5cm) piece of chain. Open the loop (Basics) on the bead unit and attach the chain. Close the loop.

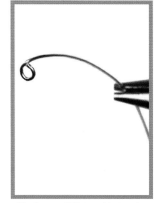

**2** Cut a 2½-in. (6.4cm) piece of wire. Bend the wire so it curves slightly. Make a plain loop at one end. Using chainnose pliers, bend the loop down so it's at a 45-degree angle from the wire.

**3** Attach the chain to the loop on the wire. Make a second earring to match the first. File the ends of the wire, if necessary.

## SupplyList

**necklace**
- **19–23** 6mm faceted rectangular lemon quartz beads (Art Gems, artgemsinc.com)
- **38–46 in.** (1–1.2m) gold-filled half-hard 24-gauge wire
- **36–42 in.** (.9–1.1m) gold-filled cable chain, 3mm links
- chainnose and roundnose pliers
- diagonal wire cutters

**earrings**
- **2** 6mm faceted rectangular lemon quartz beads
- **2** 1-in. (2.5cm) gold-filled head pins
- **5 in.** (13cm) gold-filled half-hard 22-gauge wire
- **4 in.** (10cm) gold-filled cable chain, 3mm links
- chainnose and roundnose pliers
- diagonal wire cutters
- file (optional)

# December

## Turquoise

### Physical properties

Turquoise is a relatively soft and porous stone, made of a combination of copper and iron or chromium. These elements give turquoise its distinctive shades of blue green, which can range from pure sky blue to deep grayish green. The more copper, the bluer the color and more valuable the stone. Most pieces of turquoise have black or brown veins running through them, known as a matrix. Without treatment, turquoise may discolor as it absorbs skin oils and cosmetics; most turquoise is treated to prevent this and to improve its durability. The Southwestern United States is a significant source of turquoise. Turquoise is generally affordable; imitations and synthetics abound, as well.

### History and lore

Ancient Egyptians decorated tombs and rooms with turquoise, Persian traders wore it in their turbans for protection, and the Aztecs used it to decorate ceremonial masks. Native Americans use turquoise extensively in their jewelry, and it remains one of the most universally popular stones. The bright blue color has caused many to call turquoise the stone of the sky, and it is believed to protect the wearer from evil, relieve depression, and encourage confidence.

## Blue Topaz

### Physical properties

Blue topaz ranges in color from light to medium blue and is often heat treated to get the best possible shade (silver or clear topaz can be heat treated to create blue topaz). It is reminiscent of water, and often used as a substitute for more expensive aquamarine. The stone is clear and hard, and is most frequently sold as a faceted gem for setting, or as briolette or teardrop beads.

### History and lore

Ancient civilizations believed blue topaz had a cooling effect, not only physically but mentally as well; blue topaz is believed to calm the wearer and heighten humor. Some also associate blue topaz with understanding, communication, and self-expression.

# Classic turquoise strand

String the simplest of style-conscious necklaces by alternating gumball-size turquoise rounds with tiny bicone crystals. Crystals give the appearance of little knots, lending a classic look to this choker-length piece. For the earrings, stay with gold findings to enhance the gem's warm tones. These easy pieces will take less than an hour to make.

**by Naomi Fujimoto**

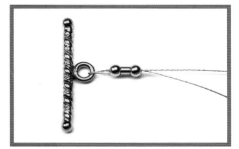

**1** necklace • Determine the finished length of your necklace. (This one is 16 in./41cm.) Add 6 in. (15cm), and cut a piece of beading wire to that length. String a round spacer, a crimp bead, a spacer, and half of a clasp. Go back through the beads and tighten the wire. Crimp the crimp bead (see Basics, p. 8), and trim the excess wire.

**2** String a bicone crystal and a turquoise bead. Repeat, alternating crystal colors, until the necklace is within 1 in. (2.5cm) of the desired length. End with a crystal.

**3** String a spacer, a crimp bead, a spacer, and the remaining clasp half. Go back through the beads just strung and tighten the wire. Check the fit and add or remove beads, if necessary. Crimp the crimp bead and trim the excess wire.

**1** earrings • String a turquoise bead on a head pin. Make a wrapped loop (Basics) above the bead.

**2** Open a jump ring (Basics) and string the dangle and an earring wire's loop. Close the jump ring. Make a second earring to match the first.

## SupplyList

**necklace**
- 16-in. (41cm) strand 11mm round turquoise beads
- **30-40** 3mm bicone crystals, in two colors (peridot satin and light colorado topaz)
- **4** 3mm round gold-filled spacer beads
- gold flexible beading wire, .014 or .015
- **2** gold-filled crimp beads
- vermeil or gold-filled toggle clasp
- chainnose or crimping pliers
- wire cutters

**earrings**
- **2** 11mm round turquoise beads, left over from necklace
- **2** 1½-in. (3.8cm) gold-filled head pins
- **2** 7mm gold-filled jump rings
- pair of gold-filled lever-back earring wires
- chainnose pliers
- roundnose pliers
- wire cutters

# Graduated turquoise disks

A richly colored strand of gemstones needs little embellishment. Keep it simple with just a few metallic accents in the front, and let the subtle flow of graduated stones move all eyes to where they belong — on you. A pair of equally subtle earrings uses the interplay between the gemstones and the accents to complete the look.

**by Rupa Balachandar**

**1** **necklace •** Determine the finished length of your necklace. (This necklace is 19 in./48cm.) Add 6 in. (15cm) and cut a piece of beading wire to that length. String: 8mm flat spacer, 18mm metal bead, 8mm spacer, largest rondelle, 8mm spacer, 18mm metal, 8mm spacer. Center the beads on the wire.

**3** On each end, string rondelles in descending size until the necklace is within 1 in. (2.5cm) of the desired length. (Set aside two of the smallest rondelles if you're planning to make matching earrings.) On each end, string: 4mm flat spacer, 3mm spacer, crimp bead, 3mm spacer, half of a clasp. Go back through the beads just strung and tighten the wire. Check the fit, and add or remove beads from each end if necessary. Crimp the crimp beads (see Basics, p. 8) and trim the excess wire.

**2** On each end, string the next largest rondelle, two 8mm spacers, the next largest rondelle, and two 8mm spacers.

**EDITOR'S TIP**
Place the gemstone strand in the groove of a design board before removing the string. This will keep the beads in a graduated order for stringing.

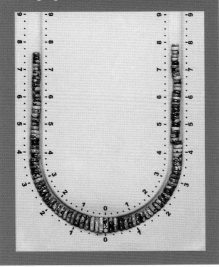

## SupplyList

**necklace**
- 16-in. (41cm) strand graduated gemstone rondelles, 6–18mm
- **2** 18mm round metal beads
- **12** 8mm flat spacers
- **2** 4mm flat spacers
- **4** 3mm spacers
- flexible beading wire, .014 or .015
- **2** crimp beads
- toggle clasp
- chainnose or crimping pliers
- wire cutters

**earrings**
- **2** 6mm rondelles, left over from necklace
- **2** 18mm round metal beads
- **2** 2-in. (5cm) head pins
- pair of earring threads
- chainnose pliers
- roundnose pliers
- wire cutters

**1** **earrings •** String a rondelle and an 18mm metal bead on a head pin. Make the first half of a wrapped loop (Basics) above the bead.

**2** Attach the dangle to the loop of an earring thread. Complete the wraps. Make a second earring to match the first.

# Blue topaz bracelet

These delicate flower shapes are reminiscent of spring, but the icy combination of blue topaz and clear crystals make this bracelet-and-earrings combination perfect for winter. You only need two simple techniques to make this eye-catching set.

**by Helene Tsigistras**

**1** bracelet • String a teardrop shaped blue topaz bead on a head pin, and make a wrapped loop (see Basics, p. 8) above the bead. Make 20 bead units.

**2** Open a jump ring (Basics), attach a lobster claw clasp to a flower component, and close the jump ring.

**3** Open a jump ring and connect the assembled end unit, two dangles, and a flower component. Close the jump ring.

**4** Continue linking two dangles and a flower component with jump rings until you are within ½ in. (1.3cm) of the desired length. End with a flower component. Open a jump ring and attach a soldered jump ring to the last component.

**1** earrings • String a teardrop on a decorative head pin, and make a wrapped loop above the bead. Make four bead units.

**2** Open a jump ring and attach two dangles and two flower components. Close jump ring.

**3** Connect two dangles and a second component with a jump ring. Open the loop (Basics) of an earring finding and attach the earring. Make a second earring to match the first.

## Supply List

**bracelet**
- **20** 5mm blue topaz teardrops
- **11** 10mm crystal flower components
- **20** 1½ in. (3.8cm) 24-gauge head pins
- **12** jump rings
- lobster claw clasp and soldered jump ring

**earrings**
- **12** 5mm blue topaz teardrops
- **8** 10mm crystal flower components
- **8** jump rings
- **4** 1½ in. (3.8cm) 24-gauge decorative head pins
- pair of earring findings

# Year-round

Birthstones don't just have significance for those born during their specified months – they also can be symbols of friends and loved ones, too. Try combining two birthstones into one piece for a beautiful and meaningful bridal shower gift, or make a special bracelet and necklace set for a mother or grandmother that features the birthstones of all her children and grandchildren.

The gemstones selected to represent each month originally were chosen because their attributes were considered to be especially beneficial during that time of the year. But no matter which month you were born in, you can enjoy wearing and sharing these stones at any time. If you like incorporating symbolism into your jewelry, you can go beyond the birthstone significance of the gemstone and look at the history and lore behind it. Make an aquamarine necklace to wear during a cruise, or a sardonyx bracelet for giving a speech. Create a necklace with changeable dangles and adjust it to fit the month, an upcoming challenge, or your mood.

Whether you were born in April or November, birthstones allow you to create beautiful, meaningful jewelry that's perfect for you or your loved ones and friends.

# Mixed-stone mother's set

**by Alicia Sandefur**

Create a beautiful bracelet featuring the birthstones, names, or initials of loved ones. A wide variety of alphabet beads are available – use beads with smooth edges for a sleek look, or block-like beads for a casual appeal. Make a separate strand to represent each child, or blend the beads together. Try the same pattern in a necklace to create a meaningful mother's set that's unique to your family.

## SupplyList

(materials will vary)
- 4.5 or 5.5mm alphabet beads
- 3 or 4mm spacer beads (one more per strand than the number of letters in each name)
- gemstones or crystals representing birth month(s)
- bead caps, spacers, and spacer bars, as desired
- 3mm spacer beads, **4** for each strand
- flexible beading wire, .014 or .015
- crimp beads, **2** for each strand
- clasp
- chainnose or crimping pliers
- wire cutters

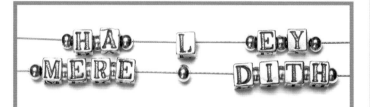

**1** For each name: Measure your wrist, add 5 in. (13cm), and cut a piece of beading wire to that length.
   String a pattern of spacer beads and alphabet blocks on each strand. Find the center point of each name and align the strands.

**2** String an assortment of gemstones, crystals, spacers, or bead caps on each end of each strand to bring the bracelet's center sections to the same length.

**3** On each side of the center section, string a spacer bar to keep the strands aligned, if desired. Continue stringing beads until the bracelet is within an inch of the desired length.

**4** Finish the bracelet with a spacer bar, if desired. String a 3mm spacer, a crimp bead, a 3mm spacer, and half of a clasp on each strand. Go back through the last beads strung, and tighten the wires. Repeat on the other end. Check the fit and add or remove beads from each end, if necessary. Crimp the crimp beads (see Basics, p. 8), and trim the excess wire.

lemon quartz

amethyst

lapis lazuli

carnelian

heliodor

clear quartz

rose quartz

### by Steven James

Change of season? Change of mood? Change the style of this easy lariat to feature timely birthstones simply by hooking different gemstones along the length of chain.

## Supply List

- 10mm gemstone for stopper bead
- **8-10** 10-30mm gemstone nuggets and **2-4** 5mm rondelles for dangles
- 2 ft. (61cm) or longer chain
- 8mm jump ring
- 4mm jump ring
- **8-10** 3mm jump rings
- **8-10** 22-gauge head pins, 3 in. (7.6cm)
- **7** in. (18cm) 22-gauge wire
- **8-10** 8mm lobster claw clasps
- chainnose and roundnose pliers
- wire cutters

**1** To make the lariat's stopper bead, string a 10mm bead on a 7-in. (18cm) piece of wire. Make the first half of a wrapped loop on each side (see Basics, p. 8).

**2** Determine the finished length of your lariat (this chain makes a 20-in./50cm loop, with a 4-in./10cm tail at the end). Cut the chain where you'd like the tail to begin.

**3** Slide the loops of your stopper bead into the end links of the short and long chain segments and complete the wraps.

**4** Open a 4mm jump ring (Basics) and attach it to the end of the short chain. Attach the 8mm jump ring to the long chain. Close the jump rings and set aside.

**7** To wear the necklace, wrap the chain around your neck and slide the short end through the 8mm jump ring. Hook a multistone dangle to the 4mm jump ring. Attach the other dangles to the chain as desired.

**5** To make the dangles, string one or more gemstones onto a head pin. Make a wrapped loop above the top bead.

**6** Use a 3mm jump ring to attach a clasp to each wrapped loop.

# Contributors

**Linda Augsburg** is Editor-at-Large for *BeadStyle* magazine and Editor of *Make It Mine* magazine. Contact her at editor@makeitminemag.com.

**Rupa Balachandar** is passionate about all things gem and jewelry related and is a regular contributor to *BeadStyle* magazine. She enjoys teaching and creating fashionable, affordable, and easy-to-make jewelry. Contact her via e-mail at info@rupab.com, or visit her Web site, rupab.com.

**Patricia Bartlein** can be reached via e-mail at patty@northwestbeads.com, or visit her Web site, northwestbeads.com.

**Paulette Biedenbender** has been beading since 1996 and owns the store Bead Needs in Hales Corners, Wis. Contact her at (414) 529-5211 or visit her Web site, beadneedsllc.com.

**Teri Bienvenue** can be contacted in care of *BeadStyle* magazine.

**Maria Camera** co-owns Bella Bella! in Milwaukee, Wis. Contact her in care of *BeadStyle* magazine.

**Naomi Fujimoto** is Senior Editor at *BeadStyle* magazine and the author of *Cool Jewels: Beading Projects for Teens*. Contact her in care of *BeadStyle*.

**Steven James** incorporates beads and jewelry making into home décor and everyday living. Visit Steven's Web site, macaroniandglitter.com.

**Jane Konkel** is Associate Editor at *BeadStyle* magazine and also indulges her crafty side as a contributor to *Make it Mine* magazine. Contact her in care of *BeadStyle*.

**Irina Miech** owns Eclectica in Brookfield, Wis. She is the author of the books *Metal Clay for Beaders*, *More Metal Clay for Beaders*, and *Inventive Metal Clay*, as well as numerous articles on beading and jewelry design projects. Contact her via e-mail at eclecticainfo@sbcglobal.net, or visit her Web site, eclecticabeads.com.

**Lea Nowicki** can be contacted in care of *BeadStyle* magazine.

**Tyrenia Pyskacek** can be reached at via e-mail at bogotabeads@aol.com.

**Alicia Sandefur** can be reached via e-mail at asandifur@aol.com.

**Brenda Schweder** is author of the book *Junk to Jewelry*, and her work also has been featured in many magazines, books, and booklets. Contact her via e-mail at b@brendaschweder.com, or visit her Web site, brendaschweder.com.

**Kathie Scrimgeour** has been a jewelry designer for over four years. Her work has been published in *BeadStyle* magazine and online in the *Bead Bugle*. Contact her via e-mail at kjscrim@yahoo.com.

**Helene Tsigistras's** jewelry has been featured in *BeadStyle* and *Bead&Button* magazines, as well as in several books. Contact her via e-mail at htsigistras@kalmbach.com.

**Diane Vickery** can be contacted in care of *BeadStyle* magazine.

**Stacey Yongue** uses wire to create a sculptural framework for incorporating beads, stones, fibers, wood, and more. Contact Stacey via e-mail at wtj@bellsouth.net, or visit her Web site, wearthisjewelry.etsy.com.